940.5472
Huber, J
Rescue
saved 7,700 allied p......
January 30-February 23,
1945, Santo Tomas Prison
Camp, Manila, Philipp

Richfield Branch Library
330-659-4343

APR 15 2021

RESCUE RAIDS OF LUZON!

RESCUE RAIDS OF LUZON!
SAVED 7,700 ALLIED PRISONERS
JANUARY 30–FEBRUARY 23, 1945

Santo Tomas Prison Camp, Manila, Philippines, WWII

JOSEPH C. HUBER JR.

authorHOUSE

AuthorHouse™
1663 Liberty Drive
Bloomington, IN 47403
www.authorhouse.com
Phone: 833-262-8899

© 2021 Joseph C. Huber Jr. All rights reserved.

No part of this book may be reproduced, stored in a retrieval system, or transmitted by any means without the written permission of the author.

Published by AuthorHouse 01/25/2021

ISBN: 978-1-6655-1417-0 (sc)
ISBN: 978-1-6655-1416-3 (hc)
ISBN: 978-1-6655-1415-6 (e)

Library of Congress Control Number: 2021901109

Print information available on the last page.

Any people depicted in stock imagery provided by Getty Images are models, and such images are being used for illustrative purposes only.
Certain stock imagery © Getty Images.

This book is printed on acid-free paper.

Because of the dynamic nature of the Internet, any web addresses or links contained in this book may have changed since publication and may no longer be valid. The views expressed in this work are solely those of the author and do not necessarily reflect the views of the publisher, and the publisher hereby disclaims any responsibility for them.

IN MEMORIAM

In memory of my parents, Joseph Casper Huber and Thelma Belle Frances Thompson Huber, whose sacrifices ensured the survival of us three children at the cost of years of their lives.

To Julia Jane McMillen Huber,
my wife, friend, and lover whom I had the good
fortune to marry on October 17, 1964, and whose help,
suggestions, and editing made this book possible.

TABLE OF CONTENTS

Preface xiii

1	Rescued 1
2	Twenty-Four Incredible Days 3
3	Sukiyaki in a Tokyo Restaurant - 1940 6
4	1940 Home Leave 12
5	Plantation Life 15
6	War 21
7	The First Camps 27
8	Happy Life Blues: The Early Months 31
9	Life at Happy Life Blues 41
10	North to Manila 46
11	Santo Tomas 50
12	Hard/Starving Times 59
13	Leyte!!! 68
14	The End and Real Starvation 74
15	January 1945, Hungry Excitement 78
16	Glorious Third of February 82
17	First Days of Freedom 89
18	The First Rescue: Cabanatuan 97
19	Surviving the February 1945 Battle of Manila 100

20	Los Baños Rescue	107
21	Summary	110
22	Going Home	111
23	Our War Lessons and Ironies	123

Epilogue 127
Appendix 1 – The Why of Japan's Actions in Their
    Great Pacific War, 1931–1945 133
Appendix 2 – Our Family's War Years Chronology 141
Notes 151

PHOTO AND ILLUSTRATION CREDITS

Front Cover – Santo Tomas Aerial View Done
 by Artist Dave Brokaw at request of author

3.1 On President Coolidge in 1940 Typhoon - Family Photo 9
3.2 Map of Philippines - March 1945 issue of Goodyear's
 Overseas News with permission 10
5.1 Huber Children on porch - Family photo 18
5.2 Company Launch - March 1945 issue of Goodyear's
 Overseas News w/p 19
5.3 Dad - Family photo 20
5.4 Part of household staff - Family photo 20
6.1 Letter - Family files 24
8.1 Sketch of Camp – Artist Dave Brokaw based on
 author's memories..33
8.2 Map of Camp - Based on author's memories 34
8.3 Our shack as sketched and given us by Father Abbitt 37
8.4 From Father Abbitt's sketch showing the area under shack.........39
11.1 Photo of Main Building - David Thompson (a
 cousin) at author's request..50
11.2 Map of Santo Tomas from MacArthur Archives 52

11.3 Arial view of Santo Tomas – Given by its owner,
Mr. Charles (Chuck) Varney 55

11.4 Our Santo Tomas shack - Photo given us by a
soldier in February, 1945 56

11.5 Barbed Wire Dad helped add to camp wall - Photo
given us in February, '45 58

12.1 Cartoon - From Fredric H. Stevens book *Santo Tomas*..............63

16.1 Sister on steps of shack - Fhoto given us by a soldier
in February 1945 84

16.2 Close-up of part of camp – portion of photo from
Chuck Varney 86

17.1 Hostages in Education Building – Getty Images 90

19.1 Family - Family photo given us by a soldier in February 1945 102

19.2 Picture on Tank – Photocopy of part of Akron
Beacon Journal front page 105

22.1 Orders - Family records 112

22.2 Entertained on Leyte - Fhoto given us by a soldier
in February 1945 116

22.3 Dock in San Francisco - Family photo 119

22.4 Train Station greeting - Akron Beacon Journal with
permission 120

22.5 In Mayflower Hotel - Akron Beacon Journal with
permission 121

E.1 LCM - Family photo..128

E.2 Huber children at front of LCM leaving the
plantation - Family photo 129

E.3 The Crister Salen - Family photo 130

PREFACE

After Japan's defeat of American/Filipino forces in 1942 in the Philippines, 25,000 US and 100,000 Filipinos surrendered, as did some 8,000 Allied civilians including our family of five. Forty thousand Filipino troops soon were dead, the rest released, while many joined the highly effective Filipino/American guerrillas.

Most American service men who survived the Bataan Death March and the horrible prison camps were shipped to slave labor, a number dying on unmarked Hell Ships of their treatment or sunk by US submarines. One in three surrendered service personnel died in captivity—most for any major American surrender. Nine out of ten survivors needed significant medical attention, many for years.

On January 10, 1944, Japan reclassified all civilian prisoners as "war prisoners," their designation for military POWs, and placed us civilians under the dreaded military police, the Kempeitai. On August 1, 1944, Japan ordered prison commandants to kill POWs if liberation appeared imminent. This happened in Palawan, Philippines, on December 14, 1944, when 157 were burned to death in a cave when the camp commandant mistook a passing US fleet for invasion.

Between January 26 and February 23 of 1945 in WWII, there was planned and executed three of the greatest raids deep into enemy territory in the Philippines to successfully rescue 7,700 starving Allied military and civilians prisoners of Japan. The first and last rescues were just 24 days apart. The astounding thing is that each raid was a hastily organized affair and each was consisted of a different set of units, brought together for that rescue, and then returned to the war. Nineteen different groups were involved, yet each raid was planned and executed in 5 days.

The driving force for the rescues was the kill order to prison commandants that no prisoners were to be allowed to survive a rescue attempt (per the order "as if they had never been there"). This tightly held secret (because its release might cause immediate killings of remaining prisoners) was evident only in the urgency with which MacArthur pressed for more rapid actions. Official histories done right after the war speak only of the pressure from above, not its primary reason. Further, another very few weeks would have seen all POWs dead by starvation.

At the start of 1945, there were fewer than 8,000 "POWs" remaining, all close to death by starvation and existing on a declining ration of 700 vitamin and protein-deficient calories. All were in Luzon and, with its January 9 invasion, the threat of their massacre became very real.

At the end of January 1945, there were 511 military POWs in Cabanatuan, some 3,760, civilian POWs and 62 Bataan/Corregidor Army nurses in Santo Tomas, 2,147 in Los Baños, civilians and 11 navy nurses and 1,340, 447 civilians POWs and 828 military prisoners in Bilibid prison. In Santo Tomas, the death rate was up to one a day and accelerating rapidly.

Many books have been written about each of the raids, and this is not an attempt to tell the whole story. Rather, this book tells the story from the perspective of one prisoner family, to provide a setting and an experience of the rescues, for a family who had ringside seats for the largest raid. It summarizes the other two raids and the rescue of the fourth camp.

The danger involved can be appreciated by the fact that the first raid took place in the midst of the main retreat corridor as the enemy moved to consolidate in the hills of Northern Luzon. The second raid rescued two camps in a city with nearly 17,000 Japanese marines and soldiers, and the third a camp in the midst of a front-line crack enemy division. Two raids required immediate evacuation of the rescued prisoners with the main raid requiring holding out till the American line could move forward to start the Battle of Manila, which saw some 120,000 people killed.

Pertinent books are listed in an appendix at the end and a brief attempt has been made to understand the cause of the terrible experiences of prisoners and Filipino civilians.

ACKNOWLEDGMENTS

I particularly wish to acknowledge two works that match my memory and also provide the Santo Tomas story before we arrived. These are Fredric H. Stevens' *Santo Tomas* and AVH Hartendorp's *The Santo Tomas Story*. Both kept illegal diaries in Santo Tomas, from which they wrote and published histories of the camp after the war.

Also of value were books by two close family friends in the camps. Helen Boyle, a missionary with many years of service in Japan until expelled just before the war, wrote *Gussie,* her story through the eyes of a dog she was keeping for her Filipino Bishop in Manila. She was one of the people who paid me to make siding from coconut fronds as an eight year old while in the Davao camp.

Father Raymond Abbitt had the shack next to ours in Davao and sketched our shack (Figures 8.3 and 8.4), our only memento of that camp. As chief cook of the Happy Life Blues Camp, he wrote briefly of the war years in his self-published biography, *A Light in the Darkness*.

Also or real value was my mother's brief autobiography which she dictated to a neighbor girl in her last years of life and which I had published as *Such a Life*.

My sister's preparation of scrapbooks of our experience with numerous letters and photos had made it possible to bring much of the story to life. I thank her both for doing it so many years ago, and for letting me keep them so that they were not destroyed in Hurricane Katrina when the 17th Street Canal Levee failed, destroying their delightful home in New Orleans's Lakeview District. Both my brother and sister offered suggestions and memories that I have included.

My father's youngest sister worked as a secretary for Goodyear Tire & Rubber Co. during the war and was the family point of contact with the Goodyear vice president for Crude Rubber. She saved copies of letters of inquiry and responses which provide a fascinating insight into the efforts of family and company to learn of our status and whereabouts during those uncertain months of captivity.

Noel Leathers, an expert on Japan, was assigned to learn Japanese and interrogated prisoners on several islands during WWII, then he served in Japan. As a former professor of history and college dean and provost at the University of Akron, his comments and insights on this book's appendix pertinent to Japan was most helpful. Perhaps the greatest value to me was his approval of the appendix and his statement that it agreed with the book he wrote.

In preparing the manuscript, I am particularly indebted to David Brokaw, who created the drawings of Davao's Happy Life Blues prison camp and the Santo Tomas prison camp; and to Tom Livigni, who brought faded WWII pictures and documents back to life.

CHAPTER 1
RESCUED

It was February 3, 1945, and I was ten and a half. Like our fellow prisoners in Santo Tomas, we were starving, my parents so weak from their sacrifices for us three children that I was the one to go across the camp for our food. We were sitting in our shack across the road from the Japanese guard barracks in the lower two floors of the Education Building when we heard a loud noise by the camp gate. Impulsively, I stepped out of our shack after curfew to go across the shantytown in the direction of a noise at the front gate and was almost shot by a guard before he turned away and I leaped back into the shack, landing hard on my right shoulder.

A little later, an even louder noise moved into our camp. With no guards about, my family ventured out onto the road between our shack and the Education Building. We children squatted barefoot, Filipino style, beside our parents on the gravel road.

Out of the gathering dust, a huge man came loping down the road, obviously not one of our fellow starving-to-the-point-of-death prisoners. Clearly a soldier, the man had a strange uniform, a helmet, and huge boots, and he carried things we had never seen—as we later learned, a walkie-talkie and an M1 carbine. Even though slightly yellow (from taking antimalarial Atabrin), he was obviously an American soldier—the first free US soldier we had seen close up since well before being taken as prisoners to our first prison camp thirty-one months earlier!

He asked Dad, "Are there any Japs around?"

Dad pointed to the Education Building and made some comment.

The soldier nodded, said something about "perimeter" and kept on running toward the edge of the camp, putting his little box to the side of his head.

The Americans had done it! Death by starvation had been thwarted. We did not know that death by a massacre of us prisoners, ordered for the next day, had also been avoided in a daring raid in which a tiny force of men had circled through enemy lines for a hundred miles to get to us.[1] We were free!

It was years before I would learn of the chain of major events, decisions, and battles on which depended the fate of our family and that of the some 7,700 remaining non-Filipino prisoners of the Japanese—and of three nearly miraculous, deep rescue raids by small ad hoc, multiservice groups that formed the last link in our survival

Everyone rescued had good reason for being in the Philippines and being captured. Dad was the manager of a Goodyear rubber plantation that produced rubber seedlings (bud grafted like roses). These were critical because they would let new Central American plantations produce the rubber America desperately needed to fight a war. We arrived in 1935, six months after I was born and had been back to America only once—in 1940, for three months home leave.

CHAPTER 2
TWENTY-FOUR INCREDIBLE DAYS

In twenty-four incredible days, small, unrelated, ad hoc groups in three daring raids deep behind enemy lines rescued doomed prisoners. All three were unbelievably successful, though none took more than five days to plan and execute and involved raids into dense concentrations of enemy troops. There were few casualties, although our camp was in the middle of the Battle for Manila after rescue, and soldiers and civilians were killed and injured there during the battle. Large-scale retaliation massacres were carried out by the Japanese near the rescued camps and in Manila.

Key was the decoding of an August 1, 1944, order from Japanese headquarters to all Japanese prison camp commanders decreeing that, if liberation looked imminent, all prisoners were to be killed "as if they had never been there." To protect unreleased prisoners, this was kept highly secret. This order was confirmed in the war crimes trials after the war and by the statement of a GI to the effect that we were supposed to be killed the next day. I took it with a grain of salt, but it indicated that word or rumor had gotten out.

Actions based on this resulted in the rescue of *all* remaining civilian and military prisoners in the Philippines, forestalling their ordered massacre. It was a rescue too late for 157 US Army prisoners of the Japanese on western

Palawan Island, who were massacred on December 14, 1944, when the camp commandant mistook a passing fleet for a rescue effort.

But all prisoners would have starved to death except for an incredible string of victories in this theater, which was considered secondary to the European for resources and manpower. Also essential were the efforts of 260,000 Filipino/American guerrillas, who provided military intelligence before and during the retaking of the Philippines and who fought as effective divisions and forces during the battles, even destroying the last Japanese tank unit.

Keys to the Philippine rescues included:

1. Battle of the Coral Sea which stopped Japan's southern advance, letting MacArthur's forces fight their way north.
2. Battle of Midway, which occurred before we went into a prison camp, happened thanks to Admiral Nimitz's risk and Joe Rochefort's brilliant intelligence work (a jealous DC office denied him promotions and medal - ultimately awarded posthumously).
3. Successful battles going north included Guadalcanal, New Guinea, Marshall and Solomon Islands, and others.
4. The battle over which to invade first, Philippines or Formosa, won by MacArthur. Formosa first would have seen all prisoners in the Philippines dead of starvation.
5. Leyte and the Battle of Leyte Gulf—the events of October, 25, 1944, when Kurita, having succeeded in breaking through to destroy the Leyte landing, unbelievably quit, did more to determine the fate of American and Allied prisoners in the Philippines than any other single minute of the war since the Battle of Midway.

RESCUE RAIDS OF LUZON!

Despite those necessary victories, it was three great raids that saved the prisoners:

1. Cabanatuan. Here, 511 military prisoners too sick and weak to be shipped out for slave labor were rescued after a thirty-mile jungle march with two guerrilla units, who blocked the main Japanese retreat route while Rangers and Alamos Scouts with a P61 twin tail fighter took care of some 250 Japanese troops. They were rescued on January 30, 1945 with the help of village people on carts drawn by carabaos (water buffalos).
2. Manila
    a. Santo Tomas. Here, 3,700 civilians and 68 army nurses were rescued after a hundred-mile drive through enemy-held territory by the First Cavalry Division with the 44th Tank Battalion, guided by guerrillas and supported continuously by Marine Air groups 32 and 24. Manila was held by 17,000 Japanese, mostly marines. Rescued on February 3, 1945.
    b. Bilibid. Here, 1,250 civilians and sick military personnel were rescued by the 37th Ohio and the 1st Cav. on February 5, 1945.
3. Los Baños. 2,147 civilians and 11 navy nurses were rescued from the midst of the crack Japanese 8th Division by the 11th Airborne with the 127th Airborne Engineering; a guerrilla unit; 11th, 511th, and 188th Parachute Infantry Regimental Combat Teams, and the 672nd Amphibious Tractor Battalion. Rescued February 23, 1946.

CHAPTER 3

SUKIYAKI IN A TOKYO RESTAURANT - 1940

Our family's story sets the tone of life and prison in those times, so different from today. Travel and mail from Akron, Ohio, to the plantation took over a month. And much of what we have today didn't exist there—like all appliances save a kerosene refrigerator.[2]

My first memory of the Japanese was a sukiyaki restaurant in Tokyo in September 1940. There was an ominous feel as our family entered from a taxi we'd taken from our ship, the luxury liner *President Coolidge*. Dad had lectured us not to stare at the high-ranking Japanese officers there and to be *very* quiet. Today, I wonder if any officers dining there were part of the group that would decide on November 1, 1940, to go to war with the United States at the end of November 1941 if their "demands" were not met. And indeed, the fleet to attack Pearl Harbor sailed on November 25, 1941.[3]

My younger siblings, Barbara and Stephen, and I followed our mother as a kimono-clad woman led us around the right edge of the main area of the restaurant up a few steps to a platform along the back, from which we took a door to a private room.

Once in the privacy of the room, we had a marvelous meal. We sat around a low table on cushions, Dad across from me beside Mom, with my siblings to my left. A young lady in a kimono kneeling at my right cooked over a fire in the middle of the table. Beside a large wok on an open fire, she placed raw ingredients in little dishes. Into the center of the wok, she would push small portions and cook the vegetables, beef, and the "seaweed" as Dad called it, and we believed him—but of course it was transparent noodles.

When it was cooked, she broke a raw egg over it. This caused me some consternation, but Dad assured me it was fine. Food was cooked and eaten in small quantities on bowls of rice while still fresh and hot. It turned out to be one of my most memorable meals. Not being familiar with chopsticks, I ate with a large spoon from the food piled on my small bowl of rice.

We had to exit past the gauntlet of tables of Japanese officers, resplendent in their dress uniforms. Covertly I peeked at them, little knowing that, in less than two years, we would be Japanese prisoners under appalling circumstances.[4] There was a real sense of relief in getting out of the restaurant and into rickshaws to go back to our safe American ship.

Japan's Pacific War was then nine years old, and the Rape of Nanking had occurred three years earlier. Japan had been embargoed by the United States in June from strategic materials and machined parts and then from aviation gasoline. The war in Europe had started a year earlier on September 1, 1939, and we were headed **back** to the

Goodyear rubber plantation in the southern Philippines for another three-year tour.

Dad's job as manager of Goodyear's Pathfinder Plantation was as critical as that of any soldier then headed for the Philippines. It was widely believed that rubber would decide the pace of the coming war. Since virtually all of the world's rubber was in the vulnerable Far East, it was estimated the war would last ten years, paced by the ability to develop an adequate safe supply of rubber.

The seedlings and seeds needed were to come from our plantation—set up when England, under the 1934 Stevenson Act, embargoed such shipments from any of their territories.[5]

After leaving Hong Kong for Manila, we encountered a typhoon, passing near its center. As the big liner (the largest on the Pacific then) began to be tossed around, Dad had us three kids get under the couch in our stateroom. Everyone was then ordered to the lounge (figure 3.1), where furniture was wedged around the edge of the room to keep it from shifting. Mom was not taking it too well, though my sister and I were happy to take an apple in lieu of a meal when the steward came by. Our eating in the storm was doing serious damage to the equilibrium of those fighting seasickness.

One lady on the upper deck claimed to be too seasick to come to the lounge. A wave smashed her cabin's thick porthole, shattering glass into her face. As I munched my apple, we watched sailors at the end of the lounge holding a cot steady against the roll of the ship while a doctor picked glass out of her face.

Figure 3.1. The lounge of the SS *President Coolidge* during a typhoon from September 22 to 29, 1940. Barbara and I are sitting up.

From Manila, we took an inter-island steamer to Zamboanga and then traveled overnight on the company's forty-foot launch the eighty miles to the Kabasalan River, next journeying thirteen miles up the river. There was no road through the jungle. The final two-mile part of the trip to the plantation from the dock was made on a carabao-pulled rail cart with canopy and seats. The map in figure 3.2 shows the location of the 2,500-acre plantation and other points of interest to this story, including Davao on the east coast of Mindanao, Baguio, Manila, the prison camps at Cabanatuan and Los Baños on Luzon, Leyte on the eastern coast midway up the chain, and Palawan Island to the west.

Clones of rubber were developed for yield and disease resistance, and trees were tapped for rubber, with employment at some three hundred. Much of the acreage was in mature trees, whose output was carefully monitored and select trees used for bud grafting. Many acres were in the seedling beds. The plantation made a first large shipment of seedlings and seeds to plantations in Panama in 1935, just after we arrived.

Figure 3.2. Map of the Philippines, with places significant to this story.

Like cultured rubber plantations around the world, Pathfinder Plantation's trees were set in a regular pattern with cover crop between them to keep down undergrowth. Rubber trees were tapped early in the morning by collecting the coagulated rubber left in the cuts from the previous tapping for a lower-grade product and then cutting a new groove a little lower down and going halfway around the tree. Late in the morning, when the latex had stopped running, it was collected, and the tree was left to rest a day.

The first seedlings were destined for the All Weather Plantation in Panama and later ones to the Speedway Plantation near Guam Lake, also in Panama. Dad worked with the botanist Dr. Bangham to develop improved rubber clones. We small children enjoyed his visits for the stories he read us, especially Billy Goat Gruff told in deep voices. Dr. Bangham had nursed the first shipments to start Central American plantations as the world moved toward war in the 1930s. In 1940, a large load of rubber seedlings and seed was sent to the Americas on returning obsolete Bolo B-18 bombers, derived from the DC-2.[6] With a seven-year cycle to significant production, these later shipments could not contribute soon to the war effort. A final shipment of 5,500 seedlings arrived by B-18 just eleven days before Pearl Harbor. Whether seedlings or crude rubber in either smoked-rib or air-dried form, all went out on the forty-foot company launch called the *Pathfinder Estate*.

Siblings Barbara and Stephen were born in 1935 and 1936 in Zamboanga. The household staff that Mom managed grew to eleven to care for us and the house, described by my father as the size of a small city block since it was also the guest house for visitors. A cousin of my mother's (also named Thelma) visited in 1935 and wrote that the living room alone could use ten 9-by-12 rugs.[7] The previous manager, who had the house built, dreamed so large and so over budget that raw lumber had to be used for the floors. Over the years, servants smoothed it by waxing the floor, skating on coconut halves with wax in the cavity.

CHAPTER 4
1940 HOME LEAVE

As Goodyear then required, we traveled first class on the largest luxury liner on the Pacific, an American Presidents Line ship. Each ocean voyage and train trip gave us a four-week vacation in quite comfortable surroundings. There was a large playroom with attendants and plenty of toys and other children to play with on the ships. We took walks on the promenade deck and explored as much of the ship as we were allowed. We sometimes saw whales and porpoises.

A steward with dinner chimes called us to meals. Only the nonstop mahjong game players (mainly Chinese) failed to drop everything for dinner. We had been raised with good table manners, so felt no qualms about dining formally. Even without the amah (nursemaid) each of us had had before this trip, we did not feel neglected.

My parents had the pleasure of cosmopolitan company and played bridge or talked after dinner when we were in bed. Like a modern cruise ship, the *President Coolidge* had shops and much to do but at a much slower pace than the frenetic one found on modern ships with people on short vacations. Each day, the staff posted our position in the ocean on a map that Dad took us to see.

RESCUE RAIDS OF LUZON!

Our stop in Hawaii was memorable, with the beach and gardens and a visit to friends of my parents who had a pool. This was shortly after the May 1940 move of the US fleet to Pearl Harbor. Once on the mainland, the three and a half-day train rides, with wonderful views and walking through a number of cars to reach the dining car, was almost as much of a delight as the rooms where the seats made up into beds and beds pulled down from the ceiling.

In Akron, after a short stay at the Mayflower Hotel, Akron's finest, we moved to a rented house in Goodyear Heights, near close relatives. Our parents took a second honeymoon while Dad's unmarried sister stayed with us. The wails of sirens in the night and the train whistles took getting used to after the plantation's quiet, but we soon learned to ignore these strange sounds.

We spent a few weeks wading and boating at a cottage on the nearby Portage Lakes, which was great, except that Dad spent a lot of time at Goodyear. This was understandable, in light of Dunkirk, the Battle of Britain and other battles in the European war, the impending Pacific War, and the desperate need for rubber seedlings and rubber. Too soon, we were back on the train and then sailing on the *President Coolidge* to return to the Philippines.

Interestingly, Japan's top admiral, Yamamoto, believed that Japan's war against the United States could result in victory only if they could win within six months, in light of the buildup Congress ordered in June/July of 1940. That window ended at the time of the battles of the Coral Sea and Midway. But neither Goodyear nor General MacArthur, then heading the Philippine/American Army, nor my parents realized that war was so eminent.

The return trip went from San Francisco to Tokyo to Yokohama to Shanghai, now controlled by the Japanese, where we tossed coins into the water by the ship and watched young children dive and recover them. Next, we went to Hong Kong and, finally, Manila.

In Manila, we stayed at the famous Manila Hotel, where General Douglas MacArthur then occupied the penthouse suite. A hired amah took us touring around the city and otherwise took care of us while our parents socialized, before returning to the isolation of the Pathfinder Plantation via an inner-island boat trip to Zamboanga and the company launch overnight to the plantation.

CHAPTER 5
PLANTATION LIFE

When we arrived back at the Pathfinder Planation, books from Calvert Home Instruction were waiting, and my mother started teaching me first grade and my siblings, kindergarten.

Mother was a granddaughter of Samuel C. Dyke, an ex-newspaper man who invented a way to make inexpensive clay marbles and started the toy and marble industry in Akron, Ohio, in the 1880s. By 1890, he was producing a million clay marbles a day and attracting a number of competing toy companies, thus making Akron the toy capital of the world. Soon, a competitor invented ways to inexpensively manufacture glass marbles, and eventually there were twenty-four glass marble companies in the area. Samuel abandoned marbles and toys and took his pottery business to Parkersburg, West Virginia.

When Mom was eleven, her parents divorced and immediately remarried others. This left her to bounce back and forth and become very self-reliant. After high school, following stints with an insurance company, as a shoe model, and dancing in riverboat shows, she went to work in the Goodyear Tire & Rubber Company Training Squad Office, where she met my father.

Dad came home for lunch and siesta, by which time Mom had managed the servants and finished our school lessons. He was the fourth of thirteen children of a handsome German immigrant, Louis Huber, born in Bavaria with a short leg, who came in steerage alone to the United States when he was fourteen. He went to work for a Pittsburgh photographer, who shot him (a Bible took the bullet and saved his life) for what he felt were my grandfather's undue attentions to his wife. Grandfather moved smartly to Akron, Ohio, where he met and married a pretty Bavarian immigrant.

Dad grew up working on his father's four-acre farm and for other farmers, becoming familiar with the care and repair of equipment. In 1918, after World War I, when he was eighteen, he and his next youngest brother bought a car and made a number of long trips, repairing the car frequently (its tires daily).

At nineteen, Dad joined Goodyear, worked his way through the Training Squad, and took a job as a first-level manager. He met Mom when he went back to visit the squad office. About that time, Goodyear opted to go into the rubber plantation business in force to assure a supply of rubber. With his farm and Squad backgrounds, Dad, then twenty-seven, was tapped to become one of the first of Goodyear's "crude rubber people." Ironically this was 1928, the year Henry Wickham, the man who'd spirited away rubber seeds from the Amazon basin of Brazil in 1876 to start rubber plantations around the world, died.

While Dad and Mom had been going together, Dad's job opportunity led to a speedy marriage just after Mom turned twenty-two, followed by a month-long honeymoon on a luxury liner to Sumatra. There, Dad helped start the creation of the sixty-four-square mile Wingfoot Plantation from primeval jungle. With Goodyear's rule that its employees travel first class, they had the largest stateroom. Those in first class with prohibition-era liquor kept it in their stateroom, where they came to enjoy their before-dinner drinks.

After a delightful hour and a half tête-à-tête with Will Rogers in Kuala Lumpur, meeting Joshua Heifetz at a reception across the strait, and a stop at Dolok Meranger (Goodyear's first purchased plantation in western Sumatra), they drove to Wingfoot Plantation in eastern Sumatra to start its development. There, they set up housekeeping in a small house with three servants for a delightful three and a half years.

When the Depression hit, the selling price of rubber dropped to half its production cost, and the plantation was closed. By skating on the edge of the Goodyear first class rules on small ships, Mom and Dad returned to Akron, sailing west around the rest of the world, stopping in Egypt, Italy, Switzerland, Paris, and England. To retain his rubber plantation expertise for the Philippine plantation, Dad was kept employed as a tire adjuster in Goodyear Tire stores till 1934, and we arrived at the plantation next to the village of Kabasalan in January 1935.

This small village was a Roman Catholic enclave between the Muslims who peopled the coast and the pagan Subanos in the hills north of the village. The Moros had their own communities, with no real allegiance to either the Philippines or the Americans. A fifteen-year war with the Moros had ended 22 years earlier, well after the United States took over the Philippines following the Spanish-American War. There was conflict between the Filipino/American guerrillas and Moros during World War II and violence there is only now subsiding.

On the plantation, when Dad returned from work, we sat on the enclosed front porch. Figure 5.1 is a view of us three children (along with the daughter of a temporary assistant manager) on one end of our long front porches, one of three large, screened porches in the house.

Joseph C. Huber Jr.

Figure 5.1. From left to right, sister Barbara, brother Stephen, the daughter of the temporary assistant manager, and myself (known then as Little Joe), all barefoot as we grew up.

Dad came home in the evenings to have a drink of Black & White Scotch and soda with Mom and relax until teatime. They sat with us while we had our tea—soup and sandwiches—and saw us off to bed. At 8:00 p.m., they and any guests had a formal dinner served by houseboys by candlelight at the big dining room table.

Guests from Zamboanga or Manila or company officials from Akron arrived frequently to spend a week or two. The launch (figure 5.2) also provided transport for villagers on a space-available basis on its weekly runs and was to be our means of escape to Australia (one of three plans) if war came.

Figure 5.2. Close-up of the company launch.

Every three months or so, we took the launch to Zamboanga. We boarded before dusk so as to be through the mangrove swamps and at sea before dark. After watching flying fish and the waves, we turned in on bunks, to waken coming into the Zamboanga docks with Basilan Island visible to the south. There where fascinating old Spanish cannons by the hotel where we stayed that we enjoyed.

Zamboanga and its surroundings had about a hundred non-Filipino families. Such a small community was close-knit, and my parents knew and visited with them in their homes or at the Army-Navy club. Visitors in turn enjoyed visiting the plantation, with its tranquility and remoteness.

The remote plantation had a very pleasant climate, which rarely dropped below 60 degrees Fahrenheit or went above 80 degrees. And because my parents were quite hospitable, we never lacked for guests. As a result, we children grew up well grounded in table and conversational manners.

The corner of the front porch of our huge one-story house is shown in figure 5.3 behind Dad with his new movie camera. Our living room held three complete sets of living room furniture, two large tables, six doors, and a wide archway and still seemed empty. It made an excellent oval track for two-wheel bicycles. Our house, like the two managers' houses, was set on eight-inch square beams of wood in a concrete bases. These provided an ideal dry, sandy play area under the house.

Figure 5.3 Dad in front of the front porch of the house in 1940.

With native amahs (nursemaids) for each child, shown with part of the rest of the staff in figure 5.4, we could rattle away in English, as well as the local corrupt Spanish, and Subano.

Figure 5.4. Part of the household staff and the three Huber children

CHAPTER 6
WAR

Despite my parent's best efforts, we were aware of the rising tensions of a possible war, clearest when the wife and infant daughter of the assistant manager returned to America in July 1941. Mom and Dad had truly married for better or worse, and Mom had no intention of taking us children to the States and leaving Dad behind. The company had suggested that women and children leave, and it's not clear whether Douglas MacArthur's urging American dependents to stay for the sake of Filipino morale had any influence on their decision.[8]

A Japanese musician came to our plantation in 1941 to give me piano and violin lessons and, I am now sure, to spy on the plantation. When he told my mother that, if she was "nice" to him, he would take care of her when the Japanese came, my father kicked him off the plantation, ending my music lessons—at no loss to music.

As concerns rose about a coming war, Dad started preparing the launch for a run to Australia, having its hull refinishing and installing a new diesel engine. Diesel fuel was laid in. Discussions were held of lining the sides and top with rubber bales, which would stop .50 caliber bullets.

After the war started, Dad had an air-raid shelter dug into the side of the hill on which the house stood. It was an open pit with a level floor. This was covered with heavy boards and several feet of dirt. The shelter had a small entrance on the downhill side.

Shortly, we were rousted out of bed to go to the air-raid shelter when planes flew overhead. Sitting on a plank laid on a shelf of dirt gave a damp earth smell on nights when airplanes were heard. Dad answered reassuringly that it would not protect us from a direct hit but would help if the planes bombed the house and that a direct hit was most unlikely. The galvanized iron roof of our city-block-sized house near the top of the hill stood out in the moonlight, but no bombs fell.

Dad had a native-style house and outbuildings built under the edge of jungle trees on the upper reaches of the Kabasalan River in the foothills. It was beside a meadow through which the river flowed. We tried a practice emergency flight, leaving suddenly carrying emergency backpacks we had prepared and hiking into the jungle.

Our hideout was delightful. Mornings and evenings, deer and small animals came to drink from the river just a few yards from our shack. In the daytime, we would go swimming in the waist-high water under the watchful eye of our houseboy, Toto. If Japanese soldiers came to the plantation, the plan was that someone would run through the rubber trees to warn us. We would grab our backpacks and make a run for the hideout. If necessary, we could even go further into the jungle up the hills.

The jungle to our north was quite rugged and so remote that the great hoax of "discovering" a previously unknown Tsaday aboriginal tribe could be realistically pulled off. The area became a haven for four headquarters of Filipino/American guerrillas on Mindanao, one of whose headquarters and a secret airfield were just sixty miles away.

Our prime planned method of escape was to get picked up by a US Navy destroyer at the mouth of the river. But of course the navy had no spare destroyers; the launch had not been refurbished in time; and, when returned to the plantation, it was given to the Filipino/American guerrillas. The jungle was the only remaining option, one that began to look very appealing.

But then, like locusts, came invaders. The American Army sent officers, who met with Dad at our house with long lists of items to requisition (a word I then learned).[9] I was entranced with their uniforms and took a sheet of paper and drew each item of kit, the Sam Browne belt, their sidearm, WWI type helmets, and so on. They took most of our medicines, most critically all our quinine, needed to combat malaria so prevalent on the island, as well as some of our canned food. Guerrillas were also given a good deal of the extra canned goods that Dad had bought just after the war began.

Refugees arrived, fleeing Zamboanga for the supposed safety of our remote plantation some eighty miles away, usually by native boat. Among them was a "remittance man," paid by his family to stay far away from home. He came fifty miles of that on foot through the jungle from the end of the nearest road and was carried in by plantation workers and dumped totally exhausted on our doorstep. Another man and a family with two small children and an elderly male relative came.

These seven refugees and five of us made a total of twelve, the assistant manager having gone to Zamboanga. Fortunately, food was not a problem, although Dad was forced to sell corn to the plantation staff, since there was not enough rice for them to buy from the company at the normal subsidized rates.

Dad bought a cow for milk and taught us children how to milk it. Our cook, Henry, sterilized the milk, and it was probably good. But it did not taste like the good canned Carnation condensed milk we grew up on.

Without quinine, necessary to combat malaria in that mosquito-infested part of the world, and since there was a baby and an elderly man, trekking through the jungle was not an option. The decision was taken to wait to be interned.

A letter (figure 6.1) was brought to the plantation by native *vinta* (an outriggered sailboat) from the Japanese commander, demanding we immediately come and surrender or face serious consequences. Dad wrote back that we had no transport and would await the arrival of Japanese forces.

Figure 6.1. Letter from the Japanese demanding we come in and surrender. (Note the error in Dad's name, as he was J. C. Huber.)

At this point, Mom said that we might as well use up the frozen, cold-storage meats, and I went with the houseboy to the cold-storage plant. Metal boxes were lifted out of the cold brine and opened, and packages of meat were put in a basket and carried back to the house.

Then, without warning, *they* came. We Huber children were wakened and moved to mattresses in our playroom to make beds available for the refugees who had been kicked out of the other houses, which were taken over by Japanese soldiers. It was June 30, 1942.

The next morning, short skinny soldiers with puttees and rifles with bayonets as long as them patrolled in front of our house. An officer with a long sword wandered about, but we were left pretty much to ourselves. Remembering the Fourth of July was coming, I made an American flag with paper and crayons and a little stick. Full of enthusiasm, I ran along the porch from where I could see the soldiers, waving my little flag. After Mom recovered from apoplexy, she grabbed me and pulled me off the porch. I got my first lecture about being a prisoner of war.

Unfazed, I made a Japanese flag based on the one their soldiers carried and started out to wave it about on the porch. This led to the second lecture, leaving me to wonder if there was anything with flags that I could do.

Early on the morning of July 3, 1942, we started our journey. We were told initially we could only take what we could carry, and Dad's rule was no toys. We kids had the knapsacks we had used to go to the jungle hideout, and our parents had a duffel bag and a suitcase. At the last minute, our parents were told they could take anything, so rolls of bedding and a meal to eat when we arrived were taken as well.

After an early breakfast, we stood waiting in front of the house with Japanese soldiers around us for what seemed like hours. Eventually, an officer came up with some official pieces of paper with English and Japanese writing, accompanied by a soldier holding a little pot of rice paste and a brush. After some interminable conversation, they closed the doors of the house and sealed it by pasting one of the pieces of paper to seal each door.

Finally we boarded a company truck for the ride to the dock. My last look at the grand house of my youth was indeed the last. The Filipinos honored the house, just as our trusted servants had hidden Mom's treasures. The great house stood empty. Even the two Japanese who came to run the plantation (and mysteriously "disappeared" within a month) used the "number two" house. A large nest of bees was found under our house, and the attempt to smoke them out was too much for the dry wood in the dry season. A grand conflagration resulted.

We rode to the dock, staring back at people as they silently watched us go by under guard. We twelve prisoners sat on our luggage on the crowded deck of the Japanese launch, a far cry from the privileged accommodation we normally got. We went around the river's bend for the ride down the Kabasalan River and through the mangrove swamp to the ocean and Zamboanga.

CHAPTER 7
THE FIRST CAMPS

While every prisoner's experiences was different, ours were reasonably typical—though our story shows what resourceful, hardworking, skilled parents can do to raise their children under such conditions. Ours provided freedom from fear and supplied the family with the best food and living conditions possible under the circumstances.

Zamboanga

We arrived in Zamboanga that evening to begin thirty-one months as prisoners in four different prison camps. We were walked under guard a few blocks to our first camp, a wooden, single-family house built on stilts. Under its one story was a tiny bodega (storeroom) on the right side at the ground level, with an open area of the left. Stairs under the middle of the house led up to the main floor.

There were already twenty-five people there, so our addition made it more crowded. A large living room was in the middle of the house, with bedrooms on both sides and a kitchen in the back middle. Helen Boyle, a missionary Japan expelled along with all Christian missionaries before the war, invited the family to move into the right rear bedroom with her fellow missionary, Naomi and a little dog, Gussie. There was just enough room for all of us to lie down to sleep.

I discovered that, apparently, no one there knew how to properly cook dry, fluffy rice in the quantities needed, and I was introduced to mushy rice—which I abhor to this day. It was probably cooked that way to avoid the loss of rice at the bottom of the pot.

The Japanese made us feed ourselves with our own money, something we were forced to do for eight months. Fortunately, Miss Boyle was fluent in Japanese and would accompany someone to go shopping, interpreting to the accompanying guard.

With nothing to do, I quickly made myself a nuisance and was banished to the dirt area on the left side below the house to play. The house was surrounded by barbed wire attached to the house posts and was guarded by a soldier, who stood on the street side. I tried talking to the guard. But since we could not understand each other, this effort did not last long.

Having exhausted the possibilities, I noticed that there were destroyed buildings nearby with only the concrete floor and low walls remaining and discovered that the barbed wire could be lifted at one corner. Since this was out of sight of our guard, I "went out under the wire."

Exploring the ruins, while keeping out of sight of the guard, I quickly found an almost new cigar box with a bright picture on the top, in which I put treasures—a spent cartridge case, a shiny token, pebbles, and a seashell. I slipped back undetected. I "broke out" a couple more times but found nothing else.

Then my sister went with me on a trip. After just one trip, during which she remembers finding a bowling pin and wondering what it was, she convinced me that we shouldn't be doing it and that it could get our family into a lot of trouble. Mom never found out.

Convent Camp in Davao

After five weeks, those in our "camp" and three more from Basilan (an island across from Zamboanga) were taken to the docks and put aboard a minesweeper. We were ordered below deck but allowed to sleep on the deck. Two days later, we arrived at Davao on eastern Mindanao, tired, dirty, and hungry. We were trucked to a place with high walls surrounding a courtyard and directed to the second floor to what appeared to be a very dirty classroom.

We were really hungry. And after an interminable wait, cornmeal mush made with cracked corn appeared, so undercooked that the bits were as hard as pebbles. Fortunately, some little cookies appeared, so we had a little to eat before eventually going to sleep on the dirty floor.

In the morning, we discovered that we were interned (a new word) in a convent school, whose nuns had been turned out. It was the Del Pilar Girls Seminary with high walls a dirt courtyard and a big wooden gate.

There were other American prisoners there, who occupied rooms on the other side of the courtyard. What interested me was that the other people knew how to cook proper rice in big cawas, an oversized wok some three feet across and nine inches deep. Unfortunately, we kept separate messes, as we had not joined our finances. Our group continued to eat mushy rice.

There were other kids there to play with and a nice tree with its trunk at a forty-five-degree angle to run up and down barefoot. One day after my brother and I ran successfully down the trunk to the ground, Barbara fell on her way down. She was not very high but was just above a cawa in which two men were roasting coffee. She landed in the cawa, knocking it and spilling the coffee. Fortunately she only burned her shoulder blade.

Dad was allowed to take her to a hospital under guard, and she remembered walking holding his hand. The burn was apparently not too bad. And since some people still had some medical supplies, she could be treated in the camp until it healed, leaving a scar to remind her of our "convent camp."

Among our fellow prisoners were ten US military nurses, one of whom had a bandaged nose. They had flown out of Bataan at the end, destined for Australia on one of two PBY-4 Catalina seaplanes. Their plane punctured a pontoon in a rough landing on a stormy Lake Lanao in northern Mindanao, damaging it so badly that the plane could not go on and injuring the nose of one of the nurses.[10] When the plane was fixed, the nurses could not be found and were left behind. I was intrigued because their uniforms had pants, like men. They were pretty.

The book *We Band of Angels* describes their story on Mindanao as part of the larger story of captured military nurses. Not too long after we arrived, they and a few others were taken away. We and they believed that they were being repatriated. Instead, they were taken to Santo Tomas Internment Camp in Manila.[11]

Having learned the word repatriated, I understood why everyone hoped for repatriation to America in exchange for Japanese prisoners of the United States. Unfortunately, except for diplomatic personnel and a few others, Japan had little interest in any captured Japanese military personnel, considering them dead and required to commit suicide.

CHAPTER 8
HAPPY LIFE BLUES: THE EARLY MONTHS

We were put on trucks with our few possessions and taken on August 23, 1942, to what we were told would be a permanent camp. After a 3.75-kilometer ride south from Davao City Hall, we came to a barbed wire enclosure next to the road. Entering, we stopped in front of a large square building, which had been a dance hall roadhouse before the war. A big sign on the building proclaimed it the "Happy Life Blues."

Tumbling out of the trucks, we lined up, and prisoners already there led us up the wide stairs under a roofed overhang in front of the building onto the main dance hall floor. At the back was a wide raised area where the band would have played. The lower building walls were wood with wood lattice above to let breezes in to cool the revelers. Above the ceiling was a galvanized iron roof, which had a propensity to leak when it rained because the building had been machine-gunned.[12] The dance floor and raised area were marked off with chalk lines into plots of four feet by seven feet for each person.

Our five spaces were two-thirds of the way back from the door and on the left side of center, about a third of the way across the dance floor from the wall. There didn't seem much to do, so I went exploring while the folks set up our area.

When I returned, our parents and others had stretched rope on short poles and suitcases and hung sheets to give us a little privacy. Getting to sleep lying on the floor in my plot next to the aisle was a problem because of all the noise. It seemed like someone was always getting up and going to or coming back from our primitive toilets, clattering in their wooden slippers (called *bakias*) on the bare wood floor. My sister remembers Mom later telling the story about a boy who walked down the hall swinging a full chamber pot on the way to the latrine. He sang, "Pee's porridge hot, pee's porridge cold," and so on.

Even when we were asleep, missionaries with an interest in astronomy would shake us kids awake to look at stars and learn the constellations. The Milky Way showed bright and brilliant in the dark sky. Even on shipboard in the middle of the Pacific Ocean, it was never more glorious.

In typical American fashion, an ad hoc committee to address immediate needs gave way to an elected governing group. Eventually an election was held and Father Joseph Franklin Ewing, a Jesuit who was the senior priest among the Jesuits was elected our head. This despite the large number of Protestant missionaries in the camp. The Jesuits formed a body of young, able-bodied men, who carried a heavy part of the camp's workload. Teams were formed for the required tasks, with Mom heading a vegetable-peeling detail in the kitchen and Dad leading one of the details that went into the surrounding jungle to cut and bring in firewood under guard.

The first job was digging latrines for the approximately three hundred of us. At first, these were pits with a pair of boards across them surrounded by a low screen. As soon as possible, multi-hole outhouses (six closely spaced, side-by-side seats cut into the planks without dividers) were built at the back of the camp, a vast improvement, even if the odor and the maggots were no better. When a little lime could be obtained, it helped a bit. With no toilet paper we used the husks of fresh coconuts.

In light of the impossibility of getting new shoes, our parents had us go barefoot, and we developed good calluses. Once, a nurse dug out a small mound of tiny pieces of gravel that had worked their way through my callus to reach the tender under skin of my foot. She said it was an eighth of an inch deep. Our feet were as good as shoes.

Separate shower facilities were built on the right front side of the compound, as seen from the road in figure 8.1 (with the plan view and key in figure 8.2). Since we had running water, the showers were good, except the water was unheated and the pressure wasn't great. In the rainy season, though, getting home with clean feet was a real problem. We would carry our bakias and wash our feet at the standpipe beside the near corner of the dance hall before putting them on.

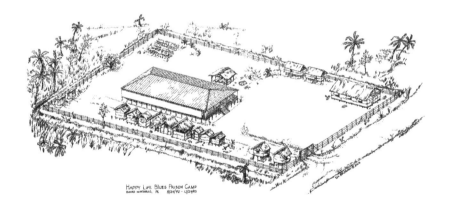

Figure 8.1 Happy Life Blues Camp. We were there from August 23, 1942, to December 24, 1943.

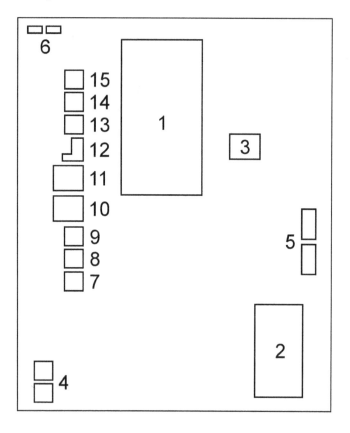

Figure 8.2. A plan view of the camp—(1) main dance hall, (2) Protestant chapel/school, (3) kitchen, (4) guard/commandant buildings, (5) showers, (6) outhouses, and (7–15) shacks. Among these, (8) was Helen Boyle's, (9) held the 'slow' boy named Johnny Apt and his caretaker, (10) was for the Jesuit priests, (11) was the Catholic chapel, (12) was the Hubers, and (13) was for Father Abbitt. Baseball was played in the open space in front.

An Episcopal priest who became our neighbor and good friend, Father Abbitt, was head of the kitchen, a thankless task in view of the fact that the Japanese made us feed ourselves and we had so little money. Men would push a cart to the nearest village to buy groceries. The camp established a survival budget of thirty-five centavos per person per day, (seventeen and a half cents in 1941 American money and three dollars in 2020). Even with no labor costs and most funds spent on food, we had to eat on the cheap.

We ate lots of tantallum greens and kang gong (spinach-like vegetables), boiled whole eggplant, and boiled sliced okra (surely boiled to maximize its glue content). A songwriter there made up a song that we children would sing when we gave entertainments: "Eggplant, oh golly gee. Okra, deliver me. I'm an American internee." Another song was about Father Abbitt's chowder.

Finally in February 1943, after eight months of feeding ourselves, the Japanese started giving us an allowance of twenty-five centavos per person per day, (twelve and a half cents American). This compares with the camp in Manila, which was funded by the Red Cross till July 18, 1942, and then provided seventy centavos per person, of which food was allocated forty-eight centavos. Of course, Manila was more expensive.

Now the camp could occasionally buy the head of a carabao. I remember going to the kitchen on an errand for my mother to see Father Abbitt and seeing a head sitting on the table covered in the large black flies that infested the garbage dump. I detest flies!

On occasion, the camp was able to buy a whole young carabao and used its blood to make blood pudding with cornmeal. It was good, and Dad had eaten it as a child growing up with his German-born parents on a farm. I especially enjoy the fried blood pudding of the Scottish version of a full English breakfast

Our Shack

Soon after we arrived, the folks decided that we needed to be off the floor and in our own house, and Dad got permission to use a small piece of land next to the main building. The ground was covered with the broken remains of many beer bottles. Everyone in the family collected glass and threw it over the fence into the ditch on the other side.

Building our shack was a do-it-yourself project, beginning with cutting down and collecting the materials from the jungle. Guards would take work parties out to cut firewood, gather materials, and get food such as bananas. As a "big kid" of eight, I was the youngest to go with Dad, then forty-two. The guards were highly amused the first time I lined up with the men for roll call, which we did before and after each excursion.

The woods started almost across the road, so we didn't have far to walk. We worked on the bigger poles first, and I would put together piles, while Dad cut them. Then we would carry them back. Dad cut down and lopped off the tops of the banana-like abaca trees, from which rope is made. We split off the fibrous outer surface for rope.

Using a swamp tree similar to a coconut tree with a hard exterior and a spongy interior, Dad would split it and remove the interior for flooring strips on the lower level. We carried back bamboo and poles, quickly amassing enough materials for the frame.

A group of the Jesuit priests who had the next lot to ours toward the gate for their chapel and living quarters came to help with the pole raising. Dad had previously notched the frame poles and tied them together with abaca. He had laid the assembled frame on the ground and dug the holes. Then, using the one nail Dad had found somewhere and bent back into shape in the ridge pole, the frames were put up and tied together, making a sturdy, yet lightweight structure that stood the test of high winds and rains that would later push over another camp building.

Mom and us children wove the coconut frond siding. Each was split, and alternate ribbed leaves were woven back through the remaining leafs before they were tied to poles, as seen in the next picture. Larger bamboo was split for the upper level flooring. Nipa for the roof had to be purchased with our dwindling money.

The drawing of our shack by Father Abbitt in figure 8.3 was from next to the fence at the back of his plot, which was the next one back from the front gate from ours. Our shack had a raised portion big enough for two beds.

On the lower level, Dad built a picnic table and benches where we could eat and where Mom could continue our lessons, which she did from memory. Next to that was the kitchen area, which was made so that it could be pushed away if it caught on fire to save the rest of the shack. On three sides of the kitchen was a waist-high bench. The side furthest from the house was packed with dirt to hold a fire, whose coals were kept burning to avoid going elsewhere to get a new fire. It was wide enough so that two fires could burn, giving Mom a "two-burner" stove.

Figure 8.3. The shack our family built at the Happy Live Blues Internment Camp.

Beneath the bedrooms was a packed earthwork area. I learned the meaning of the word awkward when I offered to help Dad tamp it down with a section of log with two upright sticks attached to its sides. When I complained that it was hard, Dad took the opportunity to explain the word awkward and left me to continue pounding.

In the background of the sketch can be seen Mount Apo, a 9,692-foot active volcano that smoked, and fortunately only smoked, the whole time we were there. It was twenty-two miles northwest of the camp. From its base under the sea, it's the world's tallest mountains at 35,410 feet.

Family Businesses

As soon as the shack was built and we moved in, our parents started the Huber Family Factory. Dad built production tooling from tin cans, bits of metal, shaped pieces of wood, and a part of a leaf spring of a car. To the top of a stump of a tree, he attached the leaf spring. He had beaten the end flat and filed sharp teeth on the curved outer end to grate coconuts.

Dad made a press to squeeze the milk out of the grated coconuts. It is shown in the center of the open space below the left side in figure 8.4. It consisted of a square tube fed from a funnel sitting over the top opening in the tube. One end was closed with perforated openings to let the milk through. In the other end, successive blocks of wood were placed and moved forward with a lever to squeeze.

Mom took the milk and simmered it in a small cawa, stirring it for hours. Eventually, clear coconut oil appeared. After it had cooled, a cloth was placed over a funnel and the oil was poured into bottles. Huber Coconut Oil was the clearest premium grade available in camp. I was proud to be part of such a fine product.

Figure 8.4. The Huber Factory on the ground beneath our shack.

The filter cloth collected a Grape-nut-like residue, little beads rich in oil, which, even when pressed out to extract every last drop of oil, yielded a very rich snack for us kids and gold miners in the camp, who asked for some to put on their cereal. When we could get white potatoes, Mom would peel and slice them thinly and fry them in our oil. We spread them out to let the oil drip off and sold them in banana leaf cones.

We made peanut butter after roasting and shelling the nuts. A spoonful gave us a bit of protein with our rice lugao for breakfast, a habit that I continue today with cereal. It helped my brother's health, since, without it, he suffered from colds and sore throats (cured after a postliberation tonsillectomy).

For our only desert, we made tapioca from cassava root. Dad peeled off the poisonous (cyanide laced) outer skin and cut it in chunks, which we kids ground in a borrowed meat grinder to get the starch-rich milk. Mom boiled it down until the little pearls of tapioca appeared.

Joseph C. Huber Jr.

I had my own business weaving coconut fronds for other people's siding. The caretaker for a "slow" teenage boy was my first customer. Then I worked for Helen Boyle and Naomi Peterson. The latter, I understood, was on the *Lusitania* when it was sunk by a German submarine in World War I before we were at war. Their shack was finished on my ninth birthday, June 16, 1943.[13] A prisoner escape from a military POW camp[i] ended our shack-building permission.[14]

Of my earnings of three pesos and sixty-five centavos, all went into the family exchequer except thirty-five centavos, which I used to buy my parents three cigarettes at the little shop in camp for Christmas 1942. They would light one after dinner, each take two puffs and put it out. Butts were then blended with other leaves and rolled into new "cigarettes" in the little canvas and wire machine that they had acquired.

CHAPTER 9
LIFE AT HAPPY LIFE BLUES

Roll Calls and Guards

Rain or shine we lined up each morning and evening for roll call. We never had an escape attempt, aside from us kids going outside the fence after chickens or for devilment. We couldn't go beyond a shallow ditch and a cleared path to let the guards observe outside the fence because of a dense growth of tall, razor-sharp, impenetrable cogon. The guards did not bother us but came to watch our plays, songfests, and baseball games. The commandant had a separate elevated shack, where Helen Boyle, our interpreter, and Father Ewing would go to hear new pronouncements or to try to negotiate improvements.

Religion

The Jesuits built a chapel next to our shack, while Protestant missionaries built a larger structure at the front of the camp opposite the gate as seen in figure 8.2 item 2. This was also used for school. Most of the children were there because missionaries did not feel it was right to send their wives and children to the United States or to abandon their parishioners.

My siblings and I took catechism lessons next door from a redheaded French-Canadian Jesuit priest who had a very low opinion of non-Catholics and who claimed, when a storm blew over the Protestant church, that it was God's hand at work. I didn't believe it, and the church/school was quickly re-erected. However, since a priest had only come to our remote village about once a year to marry, baptize, do burial rites and say Mass, for us kids this was our first real exposure to organized religion.

Education

School was in the Protestant church, with individual classes in different areas of the one room. There was very little in the way of paper, pencils, or books. In addition Mom continued our education with an emphasis on arithmetic and English. We worked hard at memorizing multiplication and division tables and spelling.

But more important than book learning were the lessons in living, coping, humor, love, and keeping a positive outlook under adversity. The worries that our folks had did not get to us, and I never heard a cross word pass between them. But like an old-fashioned farm family, we were a unit, everyone working at the appropriate level and accepting work as a given.

Without books, toys, or such things as bicycles, there was not a great deal to do in spare time. I went to the area under the main building to watch miners who played checkers there most of the day. One day in the absence of one of them, I was asked to play and came to learn the game from some very sharp players.

I remember the incredible display of the Milky Way in the dark skies, counting the Seven Sisters and the three main stars of Orion. Years later at college, Orion helped me get home after a sophomore raid on our freshman dorm room left me sans pants in the middle of a prestigious women's college miles away!

Entertainment

Since many of the missionaries were schoolteachers and singers, we children were organized into singing groups and put on skits. The guards did not seem to catch on that we always included patriotic songs, a small gesture of defiance. Having no singing voice at all, I was instructed to mouth the words but make no sound. Perhaps for the same reason, I played the nonspeaking part of victim in a skit on the Good Samaritan.

We had baseball games in which the young Jesuit priests were some of the best players. With so little else to do, they always had a good audience. With few American children on remote plantations or mission stations, it was great to have an abundance of children to play with.

Little Orphan Annie

My sister Barbara (Barb) was a real tomboy and was always getting into scrapes—so much so that Dad had two nicknames for her. The first was "Barb Wire," for her encounters with the sharp points on the barbed wire fence, and the second was "Puss on the Knee," for her knees, which were always damaged from falls and covered with scabs. Barb was of such an even disposition that it never seemed to bother her. She was, after all, a mediator and honest broker between an older and a younger brother, a role that I'm sure stood her in good stead later in life as a teacher.

One day she was presented with a baby chick, which she adored and promptly named Little Orphan Annie. She fed and fussed over it as it grew. Soon it was apparent that it was not an Annie, so Barb renamed it Little Orphan Andrew.

When it was old enough, Father Abbitt clipped a wing so that it could not fly. She would put it on its perch each night and take it down in the morning. During the day, it followed her around like a puppy.

Health

With no real access to doctors, health was, I'm sure, a real concern to our parents, who remained healthy. My brother seemed to be regularly coming down with some kind of respiratory infection. Aside from Barb's problems with her knees, she too was healthy. I was blessed with good health, except for one tooth problem. Mom also needed to see the dentist, so permission was given to accompany the buying crew into town so that we could see the dentist. The lady dentist had a foot pedal-powered dental drill, an instrument of torture that brings painful memories.

Walking back to camp with Mom, our guard, and the men from our camp pushing the cart with foodstuffs, we stopped at little stand to get something to drink, for the men probably a fermented coconut drink called tuba. A woman squatting on the ground beside the stand was selling penuche, a sticky sweet sugar from the sweepings of making sugar. Mom bought some to take back to the family.

A Real Escape

Unknown to us till years later, ten American servicemen and two Filipinos escaped from the Davao Penal Colony (DAVPECOL) on April 4, 1943.[15] This military prison camp was some thirty miles north of Davao and surrounded by a swamp. They nearly did not make it. But once they emerged from the swamp, Filipino-American guerillas fought off the pursuing Japanese and passed them from one group to another until they made their way to near our plantation, where they were picked up by the American submarine USS *Trout*.[16]

They reached America to break the story of the Bataan Death March and the abominable treatment of captured American service personnel—their purpose in escaping. Despite reluctance in high places, their horror story was finally released in January 1944 at the start of a war bond drive. Their breakout and the progress American Armed Forces were making in New Guinea and island-hopping across the Pacific undoubtedly affected our immediate future, besides ending my siding business.

The irony is that, just one year and a week after we were taken prisoner, they and an American submarine were only twenty miles from the Kabasalan River. With the Japanese sent to run the plantation having "mysteriously disappeared" in a month, and a guerrilla force stationed at the nearby village of Kabasalan within three months, had we managed to elude capture for just a little while, we too might have made the acquaintance of the submarine USS *Trout* and Australia.[17]

CHAPTER 10

NORTH TO MANILA

Life continued well for us children. We were not sleeping on the floor of the dance hall; had enough to eat; and kept busy with chores, school, play, entertainments, and watching baseball games. The efforts our parents made to create a normal family life and to raise children in such an environment were unknown to us. We knew we were loved and had no doubts that our parents loved each other. The fact that we were dirt poor was simply a fact of life. We never thought to ask for what was not possible and didn't question doing what was needed.

The impact of the Filipino/American guerrillas on our internment was also unknown to us. While we were in Davao, the Japanese made major efforts against the Mindanao guerrillas, at one time throwing 60,000 troops against them west of our camp. However, the 33,000 guerrillas on Mindanao melted into the jungles to turn on small groups of the enemy. They carried on warfare through raids, killing many Japanese and eventually restricting Japan's control of Mindanao and other major islands to major coastal cities.

In all, some 260,000 Filipinos across the islands were World War II guerrillas. They formed magnificent armies that resulted in the death of perhaps one in four of the Japanese who died in the retaking of the Philippines. It is a pity that their efforts were and are so little noted by Americans.

Despite Davao having a large prewar Japanese population and a strong garrison, a decision was made to move military and civilian prisoners and some Japanese civilians north. Most of the military prisoners had already been sent on to Japan, Formosa, and Manchuria.

At morning roll call on December 23, 1943, the camp commandant told us that we would be leaving the next day. Our shack and all the tools that Dad had made would succumb to tropical growth.

On Christmas Eve, we again stood on trucks with our small bundles. At the dock, we were taken on barges to a small Japanese freighter (one source says the *Shunsei Maru No. 1*, but I've found no confirmation) at anchor in the bay and directed into the aft hold.[18] Japanese civilians, meanwhile, were quartered in the forward part of the ship. In the hold were four rows of pairs of six-foot-wide shelves of rough planking, one about four feet above the lower level, which was just above the deck. This became home for the 306 of us for the next ten days. The two single lady missionaries, our family, and two other women shared one upper segment deck between two sets of the upright supports. It was just big enough for us to lie down to sleep—the wooden platforms luxurious compared to the hell ships our military endured.

After a good, generous meal of rice and vegetables provided by the Japanese, we sat on the planking, sang Christmas carols, and ate some fried chicken that Mom had brought with her.[19] Fifty years later, my sister and I finally realized that the treat was Little Orphan Andrew.

In the middle of the first night, my sister woke screaming when a large rat ran over her leg, and I remember telling her the rat was probably more scared of her. Since we did not see rats again, I expect that the adults took care of them.

On Christmas morning, we discovered that Santa had come to the hold of that Japanese freighter. Babs got a doll, my young brother a toy bayonet my Dad had carved, and I a homemade deck of cards. Steve's bayonet caused much consternation among our guards on deck until they realized it was a toy. I was not so old I would not have preferred the wooden toy.

With little to do, we spent a lot of time watching a nonstop Monopoly game that went on in the middle of the hold, and I played cards with the family. When allowed on the aft deck during the day, we used the outhouses, which hung over the back of the ship. There, looking through the seat, one could see the propeller-churned water. Drinking water was hot water boiled with strong ginger in a big barrel on deck. It took more than fifty years before I could again enjoy the flavor of ginger. Occasionally, Japanese guards would share some of their canned food, and I was once given a spoonful of whale meat—outstanding!

One day, in the midst of the ten-day trip, the Japanese opened up a fire hose pumping water and pointed it into the air to produce a spray to let us kids take a bath. The older boys got to wear shorts and the girls wore shifts, but younger ones had to mingle naked together under the spray. It's near the top of my most embarrassing moments.

The ship, with its plume of black smoke hugged the coast, and we could see the islands as we passed. I was unaware of the danger of American submarines. Since our ship was unmarked, our navy could not see it contained American and Allied civilian prisoners. Locked down in the aft hold, we would drown if hit by a torpedo. Had we taken a more direct open-ocean route, we would certainly have been at great risk of being killed by Americans, like those sunk on hell ships.

Fortunately, Filipino-American guerrillas had a hundred radio stations at important lookout positions throughout the islands and advised the US Navy of the sailing of Japanese ships with Americans aboard. Perhaps most importantly, they radioed vital information, leading to our victory in the Battle of the Philippine Sea, "The Great Marianas Turkey Shoot." I have not yet found proof that our safe journey came because of a message from the Filipino/American guerrillas to the navy. If so, we provided a safe passage for the Japanese civilians and soldiers traveling with us.

Docking at a Manila wharf, we were taken on trucks to the Santo Tomas Internment Camp, the new 1932 campus of the university, founded in 1611 (before the Mayflower). We dirty refugees arrived with our meager possessions, a year and two days after it had begun to function as a prison camp and joined some four thousand there.

It became a camp because leading Americans in Manila at the outbreak of the war were anxious for the safety of the civilians who would be interned. They arranged with the university that most of its buildings and land be our internment camp and presented the Japanese with a fait accompli. Thanks to typical American organizational skills, it was fully functional, despite limitations imposed by the Japanese.

CHAPTER 11
SANTO TOMAS

We tumbled off the trucks in front of the Main Building (See figure 11.1) and were herded to its right to the one-story Administration Building. Inside, it was like a production line Christmas. Dad registered us and was handed real soap, our room assignments, and our meal tickets.

Figure 11.1 The Main Building of the Santo Tomas Internment Camp (STIC) (a modern photo of the Main Building).

In our rooms, each person was assigned about seven by four feet. Dad, Steve, and I were in a room at the back of the building on the third floor for men, and Mom and Barb were in a room on the women's second floor on the right side seen from the front of the building. When we reached our rooms, we were welcomed by the elected room monitor and assigned our areas on the floor in the inner part of the room; coveted wall locations had been taken. Our first job was to take soap and towels and go to the showers and wash off grime and salt. Feeling much better, we came back and spread out our belongings.

We ate in open-air dining sheds behind the main building on long tables with benches and heard the loudspeaker give the news of the day. Dad said the speaker sounded like Don Bell, a famous anti-Japanese radio announcer before the war. He was quickly hushed and told that Bell was going by another name. It was Clarence Beliel, who'd used Don Bell as his prewar radio name.

Just eight days later, on January 10, the Japanese declared that we were now "war prisoners"—in other words POWs—and not internees, putting us in the same category as the military prisoners. In February, we were put under the Military Secret Police, the infamous Kenpeitai.[20] We were far better treated than our unfortunate servicemen, although some men from our camp were taken out and never seen again or returned much subdued. Four of our camp leaders were taken out, tortured, and killed near the end.

We hicks from Davao discovered that Santo Tomas was heaven on earth compared to the Happy Life Blues camp, like a real city. Not only did Santo Tomas have real toilet paper (two squares per trip for men, four for women) but shops, a package exchange to the outside, and better and more abundant food.

Children were enrolled in school held in rooms on the roof of the main building. Each of us was given one piece of paper and one pencil, and we were supposed to erase and reuse the paper for the school year. I still have our grades, which show that I was no scholar but was improving, finally even getting an A in English.

There were art classes, boxing lessons, and more. From my point of view, the best thing about Santo Tomas was the fact that Dad could get money and returned the money I had contributed to the family. After dinner, my sister, brother, and I would wander around the shops. Each evening until the money ran out, we would stop at a candy shop and buy a piece of hard candy for each of us. Some nights, there were movies, mostly Japanese propaganda films.

The bottom floor of the Main Building had a number of fascinating large dioramas with stuffed wild animals. A curious nine-year-old, I explored the big campus, shown in the map of figure 11.2. Next to the Administration Building (marked OFFICES) where we got new ration cards was the Education Building, which housed the Japanese guards and male prisoners. Behind the Main Building were the kitchens, which were off limits to kids.

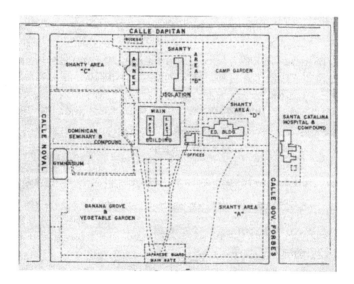

Figure 11.2. Map of Santo Tomas Internment Camp (STIC). The Administration Building is marked "OFFICES."

To the left of the Main Building, when seen from the front, was a large building that was fenced off from our part of the camp. It was occupied by the Filipino and Spanish priests from the university. Also at the left, closer to the gates, was the Gymnasium, where single men were housed. As kids, we had little reason to go there, where closely spaced cots filled the floor area we saw when we did.

At the far right was the Santa Catalina Hospital, where the army nurses from Bataan and Corregidor worked, including the ten we met at the "convent" camp in Davao. They lived as a group in the Main Building.

The courtyards in the Main Building were crowded with little shacks where people cooked and relaxed. An open-sided building was near the front gate, where bundles were exchanged. Those who had contacts in Manila could send their laundry out to be done and receive packages of food, clothes, and other necessities. Since we had no such contacts, I had no reason to be there but enjoyed watching the guards inspect the parcels and seeing the free Filipinos on the outside.

Japanese guards patrolled throughout the camp, carrying rifles with bayonets. Many were Korean and Formosan (Taiwanese) conscripts. I avoided them except for roll call, when we all lined up and were counted in an open area in front of the buildings, bowing before and after. We counted off in groups of five, in Japanese, *ichi, ni, san, chi, go* (one, two three, four, five). There were some four thousand in the camp, mostly Americans, a big city for someone who had grown up on a remote plantation near a small Filipino village.

Other kids quickly told me the story of three teenage boys who escaped shortly after the camp was started and were quickly recaptured.[21] They had been badly beaten, shot in front of camp witnesses, and buried while at least one was still alive. We were photographed in separate groups with four unrelated people. All would be shot if any in the group escaped.

We each received a Red Cross package soon after we arrived. My parents carefully saved everything nonperishable. Military prisoners and we were each supposed to receive one such package each month. The United States and the International Red Cross did their parts, and packages were sent from America once per month, only to be intercepted or forbidden entry.[22] We received one. Throughout the war, we also received only two of the monthly packages sent from Dad's parents and his siblings had regularly packed and sent.

Not long after we arrived, a group was selected to go to a new satellite camp at Los Baños, sixty miles south nearon the southern edge of large lake Laguna Del Bay. We watched several hundred, including all ten Navy nurses, board trucks with much confusion.

Shortly after we arrived, Dad borrowed money, bought, and fixed up a shack for our family to live together. It was on the main road that ran across the campus and was catty-cornered across from the corner of the Education Building, as shown in Figure 11.3.

Figure 11.4 shows the shack. This picture of the Education Building and surroundings in an aerial view was taken in fall 1945, after the shacks had been bulldozed, but a small faint gray square marks its location. The shack was near the corner of Shanty Area A (see figure 11.2) closest to the Education Building and on both the main crossroad of the camp and a path running back into Area A.

Figure 11.3. Photo of camp, taken September 1945, after conversion to a large US Army hospital and the prisoner's shacks had been bulldozed.

Shacks were originally built only for daytime use and had to be open so that guards could tell there was no canoodling going on. After we arrived, the rules were changed to permit living in the shacks to relieve pressure on the classrooms. Dad had to modify the walls, add a loft with a bed for us children, and make a kitchen area.

Figure 11.4. The Hubers' shack in Santo Tomas (distorted window had been used in the liberation and stuck back.

In addition to the loft, on the ground floor, there was a built-in bed for my parents, a picnic table where we ate our meals, and a couple of crude chairs with backs. Along the side by the path on the right, as seen from the front, there was a kitchen area where a fire could be lit on a compacted earth-covered stand. Mom planted a few of the beans we'd received from Dad's folks to grow up the side of our shack. A few weeks effort made our shack a cozy home in the middle of the world's largest war. It was a real treat not to be sleeping on the crowded floor of the cement classroom. Originally, this area was lined with trees, but as firewood became scarce, the trees were trimmed until they were bare poles.

Every able adult had to work. Mom, with her typing and shorthand skills, took a job as secretary to an elected leader of the camp. This was a great job compared to cleaning bathrooms but had a serious drawback—her boss chewed raw garlic. She took it as long as she could and then quit, taking a job in the kitchen.

Dad, despite being forty-three, took a hard labor job as a carpenter. This provided an extra ration and gave him access to much of the camp and its people. There was always something that needed fixing or building. The biggest job was to add more barbed wire to the top of the outside walls (See figure 11.5) and build an inner wall of *suwali* (a woven fabric of strips of native fiber). Anyone found between the suwali wall and the outer wall would be shot without warning. It stopped packages and notes being thrown over the wall.

Figure 11.5. Photo of added barbed wire that Dad helped put on the outer camp wall.

CHAPTER 12
HARD/STARVING TIMES

But good times ended quickly. And by June 1944, hard time with reduced rations started. *The Tribune*, a Manila Japanese propaganda newspaper that was available in camp, announced on May 24, 1944, the closing of all good restaurants to conserve rice, a sign of the food problem. It is interesting that the same issue claimed that an invasion of Europe was a long way off (D-Day occurred just days later on June 6) and that plans were underway to bomb the US West Coast. The latter probably referred to Japan's program to float thousands of gas balloons with incendiary bombs across the ocean to the United States, an effort that, fortunately, did little harm.

Our parents' struggle to keep us alive became intense. Beside their carefully hoarded food store, Mom's job in the kitchen entitled her to take home some of the potato peelings. She laboriously scraped out little bits from the inedible skins to stretch our meals—until there were no potatoes.

Dad planted, and we kids weeded a small patch of native sweet potatoes called *camotes*, not for the potatoes, for which we couldn't wait, but for the greens to boil. I heard that one man I saw being chased because he had stolen food had been a respected officer in a bank, the lesson being that the true worth of a person comes not from his or her prewar job but from how he or she dealt with adversity and considered his or her fellow man.

Until July 1944, when there was essentially no more garbage, each day the camp's pitiful garbage was taken out in fifty-gallon oil drums on a flatbed truck that drove past our shack. Enterprising men on the garbage detail had crafted false bottoms for the barrels. After the garbage was dumped, a little bit of food was hidden under the false bottoms. Discovery could lead to death, so the stakes were high, as were the sums involved. Others who were imprisoned at Santo Tomas have written of buying smuggled food.

The only part in which I was involved concerned two ducks for which Dad paid $300 dollars. This would amount to over $5,000 in 2020. They had sat in the bottom of a garbage can for the better part of a day and probably weighed no more than a pound each. We plucked and cooked them and, for a few days, had a little protein and fat. My job was to get rid of the feathers, a nightmare. Taking the feathers in a can, I waited until there were only a few people at the community garbage can. Sneaking up, I tried to shove handfuls of feather under the garbage, since we could not afford to lose the can.

It was almost impossible. The level of the garbage was almost as low as I could reach, and the feathers floated and worked their way to the surface or stuck to my hand. People came up, and everyone knew we had smuggled poultry. A woman asked what it was and how we'd gotten them. I felt guilty because I had been properly brought up and knew she and the others there were as hungry as we were.

But our family was uppermost in my mind, and I was caught on the horns of a dilemma. If they talked, the Japanese could come after us, and we might all be killed. I wanted the feathers gone! Yet at age ten, I couldn't take a totally selfish attitude and felt, and still feel, a pang that they could not be shared.

RESCUE RAIDS OF LUZON!

And we were taking a terrible risk. Dad's signature on the promissory notes, if found, would probably be enough to doom all of our family. Then near the end, the ones I thought were the smugglers were seized by the Japanese and put in a cell in the main building. The folks warned us that, if they talked or we made a slip of the tongue, the family would be in big trouble. I walked by the building and saw one of them at a window. I prayed for them and that they wouldn't talk.

We survived, so I assume that they didn't talk. They were taken out, and their bodies were found in a shallow grave, their wrists wired together behind their backs. They had been tortured and beheaded, together with three American nuns and three Filipino men. All four camp leaders deserve to be remembered, as they were trying to make the camp livable. They were Ernest Emil Johnson, Alfred Francois Duggleby, Clifford Lawrence Larson, and Carroll Calkins Grinnel, chairman of the elected internee committee.[23]

My parents said that camp experience proved one's moral fiber. Many who did not rank high in the eyes of others for their morals in other areas proved themselves to be absolutely virtuous of other's food and belongings and caring for others while starving.

Dad's hard physical labor for the Japanese earned him a badly needed extra food ration. Mom scrupulously divided all our food into five absolutely equal portions, which meant that our parents and Dad in particular were sacrificing their weight and health so that we children would benefit. By mid-January 1945, Dad developed beriberi and had to quit work. But his extra ration, whether it was 900 or 800 or eventually less than 700 calories a day, provided an extra margin, at great expense in labor from a starving man. The Japanese counted children as due a half ration, a distinction the camp did not make.

Most of the events that led to saving both the lives of the almost eight thousand remaining allied prisoners in the Philippines occurred in 1944.

A key was Admiral Halsey's great raid against the Japanese air strength on Formosa, in which over five hundred Japanese planes were destroyed, thus assuring that the Philippines could not be resupplied to foil the US invasion. The Formosa raid set the stage for MacArthur's return, and Halsey suggested that the invasion be advanced by a month. MacArthur agreed and moved the invasion date up a month to October 20, 1944. Based on intelligence decrypts of Japanese communications that showed most enemy forces were concentrated on the northern island of Luzon, he moved the invasion site from southern Mindanao north to Leyte.

Then decrypts of Japanese encoded traffic and intelligence supplied by the Philippine guerrillas led to the Great Marianas Turkey Shoot, which crippled Japan's naval aviation and assured it could not effectively interfere.

As the oldest child and fed the same as my parents, at ten, I was in the better shape and went to get the family rations from the kitchen, particularly after the camp decided that raw rice would no longer be handed out for rations, and all would eat the lugao (watery rice with a few beans or kernels of corn or camotes) cooked in the camp kitchen.

The first air raid on September 21, 1944, gave us great hope. It did, however, create a danger from shrapnel raining down from Japanese antiaircraft guns. Our parents assured us that the Americans knew where we were and would not bomb us. On December 23, the danger of shrapnel caused school to be canceled. Of course our declining diet made climbing the stairs to the fourth floor much harder, and the effort and consumed body fat we did not have.

Shrapnel was more than just a mild concern, since a piece passed between my sister and my legs as we sat together on our bed in the loft. Another hit Mom's chair just after she got up. Before the first air raid, the Japanese camp commandant had recommended that air-raid shelters be built for those not in the concrete buildings. Dad somehow dredged up the energy to build us a tiny air-raid shelter, using blocks of sod. He

RESCUE RAIDS OF LUZON!

cut a hole in the floor near their bed for an entrance and built it under the bed with a layer of sod on the floor for a top.

The shelter worked, and we were safe, though twice shrapnel came through the entrance to land safely on the shelter's dirt floor. One piece of shrapnel came past my arm, and later, a piece passed very close to my sister's arm. I tried to pick it up, to discover that newly made shrapnel is very hot.

Bombings began in earnest after that first glorious day. Occasionally, then more and more frequently, American planes appeared overhead, and the camp commandant insisted we stay indoors and not look. Soon, Japanese airplanes were leaving early every morning, their distinctive-sounding engines reminding us for all the world of sewing machines. At dusk, after the American planes had gone, they would return. It became our family joke to comment on the "sewing machines" skedaddling and creeping back at dusk. It gave us a good feeling that the Japanese did not seem so powerful.

We returned to cooking in the shanty on October 4, on a ration that consisted of a mixture of rice with a few camotes, beans, and corn. Protein of any kind was virtually nonexistent, except for beans and the worms in the rice. The impact of food is perhaps best illustrated by the cartoon from Stevens's book in figure 12.1.

Figure 12.1. Copy of a chalk cartoon for Thanksgiving Day, one of those drawn daily near the food line. (From Stevens's book *Santo Tomas Internment Camp*)

While food was our main concern, our parents kept life on an even keel, to the extent that curfews and regular roll calls can be said to be normal. We were taught the proper way to bow and, after counting off, to make the deep bow to our guards. One day, the Japanese lieutenant decided we were getting sloppy and, for several days, kept us an interminable time practicing in the hot sun.

While air raids were the high points of hope, exhilarating and moving, starvation was ever present. Since our shanty was located on the road to the hospital, we saw more and more trips by a cart drawn by a starving horse carrying bodies wrapped in suwali going from the hospital toward the main building to then turn and go out the main gate. At first it was every few days and then every other day, eventually almost daily.

As time went on, there would be two bodies. I looked whenever I heard the sound of the horse clip-clopping on the road yet could feel nothing for the unknown people whose bodies were being taken away.

Deaths resulted from starvation or starvation-aided illness, for which our doctors had no medicines (Red Cross medicines intended for us were taken by the Japanese). For the last four months, the grim totals in a camp of just over 3,700 mostly young people were:[24]

Month	Deaths
October 1944	13
November 1944	17
December 1944	20
January 1945	34

After liberation, sixty-five were too far over the edge of starvation to recover, even with food and medicines, and died in the next eleven days. How many more would have died had we not started to get more food by February 4? After the war, Dad told his relatives that, at the end, he believed that, in another two weeks, our family would go over the edge of starvation.

Each meal, no matter what "slop" it was, became a major event that we looked forward to. We would take our bowl and spoon and eat it in tiny bites, chewing each bit of soft lugao as if it were tough steak. Then having scraped the dish till every grain was gone, we would thoroughly lick our spoons. Setting the spoons down we would pick up the plate and lick every scrap of remnant and bit of moisture that remained. When we finished, plate and spoon compared favorably to the proverbial hound's tooth. And we were still hungry. Our shrunken bellies were full, but we had the gnawing pang that one experiences after fasting following a big meal. We knew there was no more food until the next meal.

Food only seemed to lead to tragedy. The camp crop of kangkong, a leafy vegetable not unlike camote greens, failed on October 6, 1944, due to a lack of rain. Somewhere near the end, I had a catastrophe washing rice for Mom. I took it to the standpipe that stood on our corner of the lawn in front of the Education Building, where the Japanese guards lived on the first floor. I was to remove the stones and dirt and debris left by insects. Worms were okay, since they provided protein. I tried to turn the water on slowly to run over the rice, but it came with a blast, splattering rice grains all over the mud under the standpipe.

Heartsick, I worked for what seemed an eternity trying to recover the rice. I tried picking up handfuls of mud and rice to pick out the rice. But since I chewed my nails, my efforts to pick up the grains yielded almost nothing. In utter frustration, knowing Mom needed the rice to cook, I walked back to the shanty and confessed my stupidity. To my eternal regret, I must have lost at least a tablespoon of raw rice, perhaps enough to give each of us another tablespoon of lugao.

There was no fuel to be burned for heat, and on cool Manila nights in the winter of 1944/45, we had to bundle up or go to bed. I remember Mom and Babs sitting in our little front area with blankets around them to keep warm. Of course the fact that we had virtually no body fat meant we had no natural insulation and cold was particularly penetrating.

Recipes became a main occupation for many. Men in the Education Building talked lovingly of recipes they remembered. In infinite detail, they would describe each ingredient, how it was cooked, and what it tasted like. We kids would sit at their feet as they sat on the steps and listen to them tell of these wondrous things—like kids listening to adventure stories, only these were much better. Best remembered were their discussions of roasting a turkey and its dressing—whether it should be made with or without oysters (whatever they were) or chestnuts, white bread or cornbread; casseroles; elaborate French dishes with sauces; and all sorts of meat dishes, from meatloaf to lamb and roast beef. They also described Rice Taffel (rijsttafel in Dutch) that had over fifty different dishes. Each recipe and every cooking step was described. A recipe book of such recipes written by World War II military prisoners at Bilibid Prison, just three long blocks away, rings true to those heard sitting at the foot of the steps.

As our family sat in our shanty in the evenings, we would sometimes talk about the food we most wanted. Dad just wanted a glass of cider vinegar like the kind he had when a boy in Tallmadge, Ohio. Mom wanted a plain cold, boiled potato, and I could taste it just thinking about it. I would dream of eating it one tiny bite at a time. But what I really wanted was plain boiled white rice, not lugao. We had forgotten what fresh meat and fish tasted like. Our only meat was from tins that Mom opened at too-long intervals and mixed in our food for the few days she could make it last without spoiling.

But food was not the only thing in our lives. Air raids were a regular occurrence and did much to keep up our spirits. While we had full confidence that the American flyers knew exactly where our camp was and would avoid bombing us, eventually the Japanese also came to the same realization and began using the camp as a storage area.

The area in front of the Education Building and catty-corner across the street from our shack had been an assembly and inspection area for the guards. Then, as food became scarce, the guards made it into a garden, and we watched soldiers plant and till, dressed in their "G- strings." Now it was piled with supplies, including bales of rubber like we made on the plantation. I looked but could not see any with our plantation's markings. Other Japanese supplies were stored by the front gate.

More Japanese soldiers moved into camp and took over half of the second floor of the Education Building. But even they and we were not totally safe. Bullets hit the hospital (December 14, 1944), and a patient was wounded.[25]

While we could not see over the walls, we could hear a lot of noise. The Japanese were out of both gas and tires. Trucks used charcoal burners to make fuel to use in the engines, belching black smoke. Without tires, they ran on rims, sounding like tanks.

Roll calls continued twice a day, and searches were made on a regular basis. They were searching for the homemade transmitter and receiver that internees had built and hidden against the day they might be needed. The receiver had been used regularly and supported the camp rumor mills.

CHAPTER 13
LEYTE!!!

The next set of events essential to the survival of the remaining prisoners took place on the islands and nearby waters of the central Philippines.[26] When Leyte was invaded at the city of Tacloban on October 20, 1944, we heard right away. It led to the famous picture of MacArthur wading through the water to "return" to the Philippines, actually a second time because, on the first, the water was too deep, and he needed to change into a clean uniform for the photo.

On the day after the landing, announcements being made by "Don Bell" included one about some rations being delayed. At the conclusion, we clearly heard him say, "It's better late-ay than never." Everyone laughed because the rumor was all over camp about the landing on Leyte, pronounced /lay-tay/.

It was a big lift to our hopes and expectations. But bodies continued to go out on the horse-drawn cart at an increased rate, and illness and starvation might overtake us before the American Army could rescue us. As a kid, I had no doubt about surviving, a testament to our parents. Adults also worried about massacres and atrocities.

Our delight was in the fact that American forces had finally reached the Philippines. Eventually they would get to whomever of us were left.

In a logistic miracle involving ships all over the Pacific, schedules had been advanced a month and a landing made on Leyte just five weeks after the decision, crucial timing.

Following the Leyte landing, under intense pressure from the high command in Tokyo, General Takahashi, the conqueror of Malaysia and Singapore, changed his plans and proceeded to make a stand on Leyte, seriously jeopardizing his plan to fight a delaying war of maneuver on Luzon—as MacArthur had originally planned at the beginning of the war. Fierce fighting for the island of Leyte was aided by intelligence decrypts that gave information that permitted the United States to destroy men and supplies being ferried to Leyte.

Equally important to our survival were other decrypts that revealed the resulting declining Japanese strength on Luzon, permitting MacArthur to proceed expeditiously with the Luzon landings, delayed by only nine increasingly important days.

Of these events, though, the most important to our survival was the naval Battle of Leyte Gulf, fought October 23–26, 1944. It was the largest naval battle the world has ever seen, or will ever see. This action, in four parts, included Halsey's famous dash after, and the eventual destruction of the toothless Japanese carriers who had lost their aircraft in the Great Marianas Turkey Shoot (the Battle of the Philippine Sea). This fleet, under Admiral Osawa, was acting as a decoy to draw Halsey away from the landing site so that the Japanese surface navy could decimate our forces and destroy the critically needed materials there.

American forces were equally successful against the southern Japanese pincer movement in the Battle of the Surigao Strait. Here, for the last time ever, American Admiral Jesse Oldendorf fulfilled every naval officer's dream of crossing the T with capital ships. A force of fourteen heavy ships, including five Pearl Harbor battleships, sailed in line of battle, while three Japanese capital ships, having successfully survived PT attacks, sailed in to form the vertical line of the T. In this arrangement, the Japanese force came one at a time to take the full fury of all the American ships forward and aft batteries while able to use only their forward guns. Unbelievably, despite many hits, no Japanese ships were sunk, and destroyers with torpedoes had to finish the job.

Before Halsey was decoyed away, his carrier planes made a telling attack on the main Japanese northern pincer's thrust through the Sibuyan Sea northwest of Leyte, sinking the *Musashi*, one of two Japanese super-battleships, and forcing Admiral Kurita to turn around.

But while Halsey chased north after the Japanese carriers, he left the critical San Bernardino Strait north of Leyte, without even a picket destroyer. Kurita reversed course during the night and found a clear path to the landing site. At 6:48 a.m., he achieved complete surprise!

The only force standing in his way to the landing site was Taffy 3, a small landing support group of six small "jeep" carriers (merchant ships topped by a small flight deck), three destroyers, and four small anti-submarine destroyer escorts. Their total tonnage was less than that of Kurita's remaining super-battleship and flagship, the Yamato, their heaviest guns 6 inchers compared to the 18.1-inch guns of the *Yamato's* main battery and the 8- and 14-inch guns of Kurita's cruisers and other battleships.

Taffy 3 was commanded by Admiral Ziggy (Clifton A. F.) Sprague, a hero at Pearl Harbor, where he commanded the ammunition ship *Tangier*, one of the few to engage the attacking aircraft. During the attack, he'd stood calmly exposed on the bridge, an inspiration to his sailors who knew that a hit on the *Tangier* would destroy the ship and a large chunk of Pearl Harbor.

Off the island of Samar north of Leyte, the two fleets discovered each other when, just twenty miles apart, steaming on a collision course. Ziggy's small carrier's planes were armed for close air support to ground

RESCUE RAIDS OF LUZON!

troops fighting on Leyte, not attacking capital ships. Now, just as Oldendorf had achieved the battleship commander's dream of crossing the T, Kurita found himself in every gun admiral's dream of having carriers in range as 150-foot-high, colored splashes from large shells fell among Ziggy's jeep carriers. It should have been a massacre. Or Kurita should have brushed by them, leaving a couple of cruisers and a few destroyers to deal with them.

But with daring, brilliance, and the incredible bravery of thousands of sailors, Taffy 3 used smoke, thunder squalls, ballet-precision joint maneuvering, nuisance air attacks, and incredible torpedo charges by destroyers and destroyer escorts into the teeth of the Japanese fleet to keep the force alive. It caused Kurita to ignore his mission and concentrate on their tiny force. Taffy 3 sent all available planes aloft to harass Kurita. And when low on gas, they landed at Tacloban without warning to refuel and rearm, unnerving US Army men.

Ziggy's jeep carriers were scoring hits on Japanese cruisers (the *White Plains* scored six hits), and a gunner joked that they nearly sucked them close enough to hit them with their 40 mm cannons. One carrier even took a nonlethal hit from a fourteen-inch gun, which passed through its thin skin without exploding—the only carrier ever to be so hit.

With American air attacks swarming like bees around his ships, even though our planes were without adequate bombs and, in some cases, even without bullets for their guns, Kurita ordered his ships to take individual action, appropriate for air attacks.

Eventually the enemy closed in on three sides of Ziggy's flotilla. In another few minutes, he would see Taffy 3 decimated. The carrier *Gambier Bay* had been slowed and was sunk by a swarm of Japanese ships. *Roberts*, a destroyer escort, and two destroyers, the *Hoel* and the *Johnson*, were sunk making their torpedo attacks into the Japanese squadrons of cruisers and battleships. Even Kurita on the *Yamato* reversed course away from the battle to avoid torpedoes.

Kurita was finally free to fulfill his mission against the Leyte beachhead! Ziggy had bought over two hours and was finished. This historic, classic battle was ending, though after the battle they lost the jeep carrier San Lo, the first loss of a major ship to kamikaze attacks. Due to a reporting error, her sailors spent over fifty hours in the water. But another force of jeep carriers, Taffy 2, finally got aircraft with torpedoes to the scene. This may have helped convince Kurita that he was up against fleet carriers. **In any event, Kurita quit!**

At 9:11 a.m., he ordered withdrawal! This, despite the fact that his attack was intended to be a suicide mission. It was against the advice of his commanders and despite the fact that his fleet was intact. Even if the whole task force would be lost, it would have seriously set back the US liberation of the Philippines and let Japanese forces better defend the island of Leyte.

Japan's terrible losses at Surigao and to Osawa's decoy fleet had been in vain and the landing untouched. An artillery man who was then at Tacloban said years later that his group were frantically cutting down trees to be able to bring their puny ordinance to bear on the *Yamato* and other major ships bearing down on them. Their 155 mm ordinance was all that stood in the way of Kurita's big guns.

Kurita had failed, and Halsey's reputation was rescued from being responsible for the destruction of the Tacloban landing on Leyte by leaving the San Bernardino Strait open and in being slow to respond to Ziggy's plain voice calls for assistance. He also lost the chance to be the admiral to fight the world's last battleship battle. He could have if he'd either left a force of battleships at the San Bernardino Straits, as he had proposed, or when he'd finally sent a battleship force south, had them move faster than a leisurely twenty knots. As a result, the battleship force missed by three hours the chance to engage the retreating Kurita.

The events of October 25, 1944, did more to determine the fate of American and Allied prisoners in the Philippines than any other single day of the war since the Battle of Midway. If Kurita had succeeded against the Tacloban landing site and its mountains of supplies, the pace of war in the Philippines would have been set back by fatal months. No Allied POWs would have survived. The battle was over long before we knew it had been fought.

CHAPTER 14
THE END AND REAL STARVATION

American planes would come over any time of the day they chose, facing only antiaircraft guns. Our first sighting of the humongous four-engine bombers (B-29s) on December 23, 1944 was awe inspiring. They were immense compared to any planes we had ever seen. Their sheer size fed our need to believe in liberation, though I was sad when one was hit (January 8, 1945) and went down trailing smoke. Parachutes came out and I prayed that they all made it. Much later, I learned that they all got down safely, only to be beheaded for daring to attack the Japanese, as did many other American airmen downed over Japanese-held areas.

With hunger a never-forgotten companion, though, food was our focus. Nothing was wasted, so much so that I still cringe a bit when leaving food on a plate. Christmas of 1944 was a nonevent. Despite clear memories of the concentration camp Christmases of 1942 and 1943, only two memories of 1944 remain. One was that each of us kids received a piece of hard candy and a banana from the camp. My folks refused to share my piece of candy, and I felt guilty eating it myself and went off to do so in private.

The second was our feast. Our family and four others combined our three bananas and hoarded scraps to make a "fruit cake." It was the size of a cupcake, to be divided equally among nine people. I reveled in my piece and, to this day, enjoy fruitcake, which, of course, is far richer than ours made with cassava flour and scraps.

From the camp records, we went down briefly to two meals a day on December 23, 1944—breakfast at 8:30 and dinner at 4:00. Mom divided our rations to spread it out to three meals and, for us kids, a bedtime snack of a couple of spoonfulls of watery lugao.

On the first day of the New Year, I started a diary in a little notebook, which was my Christmas present. There was little to put in it besides what we had to eat for each meal, the weather, the air raids, and what the Japanese guards were doing. It was taken by the American Army censors and returned many months later, only to disappear in postwar moves.

On January 4, 1945, the daily cereal allowance for the camp of over 3,700 was cut to 550 kilos (1,210 pounds) to go with some camotes. That gave each of us 2.6 ounces for each of two meals, whereas a healthy adult needs three to four pounds of food a day.[27] The diet was grossly deficient in protein. Fruit and vegetables were native leaf vegetables like camote leaves and kangkong. We were dwindling fast, as our bodies were consuming themselves and our stomachs shrinking.

The records also make clear the real effects. Weight losses between January 1942 when Santo Tomas camp was established and July 1944 were thirty-one pounds for men and eighteen pounds for women. A good part of this weight loss took place in the first six months of 1944.[28]

From this now lean weight, the additional weight losses till January 20, 1945, were twenty pounds for men and fourteen pounds for women. The calorie record supports this going from a sustaining diet of 2,076 calories per day in March 1944 to 1,402 calories per day in October 1944 to a final level of around 600 calories per day.

The menus at the end support this starvation:[29]

December 15, 1944
- o   Breakfast   Emergency biscuit
- o   Lunch   Ladle of lugao
- o   Dinner   Ladle of lugao, ladle of gravy

December 30, 1944
- o   Breakfast   Ladle of lugao
- o   Lunch   Ladle vegetable stock
- o   Dinner   Ladle of boiled camotes, ladle of gravy

January 13, 1945 (When I picked up our family's rations I watched the server carefully scraping the top of the ladle flat and running his utensil around its bottom to make sure none could drop off the bottom, giving someone a larger serving.)

- o   Breakfast   Smaller ladle of watery lugao
- o   Lunch   Same, smaller ladle leveled off of soy bean soup
- o   Dinner   Ladle of camote, bean, and rice stew (i.e. lugao)

Through January, rations continued to be cut, and more and more of the calories were in watery lugao. If not for hoarded food that the folks reluctantly dipped into, we would have been in very serious shape.

For January 26, 1945, the allowance was only two ounces of uncooked food per meal per person. Of this, 80 percent was cereal and only 20 percent was beans. And the two-ounce figure was gross weight with short weight bags, spoilage, and losses in cooking and distribution reducing the amount that reached our stomachs.

We had only one can of meat remaining from our Red Cross package and food reserves. The only things that had kept us going earlier were our parents' decision to provide food for us children and enough for them to survive to care for us and their turning to the smugglers. Our parents were willing to risk their lives and sign huge promissory notes for postwar repayment for food received. With all the lawyers interned, these notes were ironclad—to the smugglers or to their heirs.

CHAPTER 15
JANUARY 1945, HUNGRY EXCITEMENT

On January 6, guards began to burn records and gave signs of leaving. Supplies from in front of the Education Building were moved out the next day. The Japanese Army's Philippine commander, General Yamashito, had ordered that Manila be declared an open city, just as MacArthur had done in 1941. He planned to concentrate his troops and supplies in the mountainous central and northern Luzon to fight in the mountains and to prolong the defense as long as possible and delay the attack on Japan. But he later agreed to let the stores at the Manila docks be defended![30]

The Japanese Navy, historically at loggerheads with the Japanese Army, was led in Manila by Marine Admiral Iwabuci, who commanded thirteen thousand marines and had authority over an additional three thousand soldiers. He was determined to make the taking of Manila a bloodbath for the Americans by fighting to the last man. He had lost a ship and, to his shame under the Bushido code, had failed to go down with it.[31] Now he could reclaim his honor with a fight to the death. He cared nothing for the Filipino civilians or the sacrifice of his men or himself. Hitler was not the only one to talk of defending cities to the last man. To his credit, and unlike Admiral Kurita, if any credit there be, he included himself, apparently by suicide.

In Santo Tomas, the admiral's stand led to the guards staying. When American fighter planes flew low over the camp, we could only wave if there were no guards around. But we could, for the first time, actually see free American flyers in the cockpits!

Life continued as before. According to a camp schedule in Frederic Steven's book on Santo Tomas, a typical day went as follows, using the January 15, 1945, schedule and my recollections.

- **7:00 a.m.—Reveille.** Over the public address system came the sounds of a recording of an American song. Best remembered, "You're in the army now. You're not behind a plow. You gotta get up, you gotta get up, you gotta get up in the morning."
- **8:00 – 9:30** *a.m.*—**Roll Call**. I recall that the guards had platforms built in front of the places we lined up for roll call, but can find no record of this.

    Our place for roll call was the open field in front of the yard of the Education Building. We lined up and waited while the count went on and was double-checked and reported and reported and reported. Eventually those who were weak were allowed to bring chairs (January 20, 1945) but were required to stand during counting. Mom and Dad brought chairs.
- **9:30** *a.m.*—**Breakfast**. I would go to get breakfast for our family and bring it back to the shack. After we ate, we would do something quiet because we had so little energy. We children would wander about and talk to other kids or go to listen to old men describing recipes.

- o **Lunch**. Lunch was little lugao saved from breakfast. After lunch. the folks had siesta, and we were quiet.
- o **4:00 p.m.—Dinner**. We would sit around and do mental exercises, such as practice the multiplication tables and sometimes talk about foods we wanted.
- o **5:30–6:30** *p.m.*—**Roll call**. Again.
- o **7:00** *p.m.*—**Lights out and curfew**. Just before lights out, we children would eat the little cold lugao mom had saved for us.

As starvation took its toll, the doctors of our camp were hauled into the commandant's office and told to change the death certificates they had submitted. They refused to do so and were put in a locked room in the main building. Of course, deaths by starvation did not stop, but the Japanese commandant may have felt worried about justice after the war. More and more bodies were pulled past our shanty by the horse as skinny as we were.

During the early years at Santo Tomas before we arrived, mortality held steady at about 2 percent, not unreasonable for a well-off population that contained all ages but few infants. Besides, babies require women to have body fat and men whose sex drive hasn't been turned off by starvation. Now, women stopped menstruating, becoming infertile, and men thought of recipes. As starvation deepened, the death rate began to take off.

We had ringside seats for all the commotion in front of the Education Building with the guards doing daily calisthenics in their G-strings. It gave us something to do. We watched their inspection of the guards, and I saw one soldier being brutally slapped repeatedly by an officer in front of the whole group, something I could not understand.

On January 6, as I was coming back from a trip to the latrines, a guard called and motioned me over where he was burning things in front of the Education Building. I came and gave him the required bow, and he handed me a decorated wooden rattle. Thanking him (abrigatou) several times, bowing each time, I went back to the shack to show it to my parents and immediately sketched it in my diary.

Even then I knew it was something he had bought for his own very young child. I now believe he guessed he would not live long. I was touched by his gift. Indeed, he and all but 330 of the Japanese marines and soldiers defending Manila under Admiral Iwabuci would be dead by March 3. He may have been a conscripted Korean or Formosan (Taiwanese), although the Korean guards were larger.

As January ended, we could, for the first time, hear the distant sounds of big guns or explosions. Along with the burning of papers, there was much commotion in the Japanese ranks. But the guards were still there.

CHAPTER 16
GLORIOUS THIRD OF FEBRUARY

It was well we didn't know our chances of survival were even slimmer than we thought. On August 1, 1944, Allied intelligence intercepted and decoded a general order from the Japanese War Ministry in Tokyo to all prison camp commandants, instructing them that "all prisoners were to be executed when their release was imminent."[32] Its English translation reads, "In any case, the aim is to annihilate them all and not to leave any traces." Despite Japanese attempts to burn all copies, some were found and included in the record of the war crime trials held after World War II.

It was not an idle order and was carried out on December 14, 1944. On that day, 157 were burned to death in air-raid shelters on Palawan Island in the southwestern Philippines. The last survivor of the handful who escaped died in 2010. That commandant had mistaken passing ships for an invasion force.

Even before the order was issued, ninety-eight had been massacred on Wake Island on May 10, 1943. Just before the end of the war in Malaysia, all but six of two thousand Australian POWs died in a death march meant to get rid of them (the survivors escaped with the aid of the local population).[33]

This was unknown to us, although there are hints in early published books that our camp leaders who had access to the homemade hidden

RESCUE RAIDS OF LUZON!

radio knew and were concerned enough to make plans of what to do in that event. American forces were trying hard to quickly reach the remaining Allied prisoners in the Philippines "before they might be killed."—all together 7,700 souls.

On February 1, the Japanese soldiers in our camp killed all their animals, and camp leaders could sense that something was up. The whole camp was still in an uproar over the jailed doctors. When it was quiet, we could hear the sounds of Japanese trucks running on their rims.

It was quiet most of the day of February 2, though the guards were agitated. Before curfew and after roll call, on the advice of another kid who said you could see fires from there, some of us kids made our way to the roof of the Main Building next to our former classrooms.

From the back of the building, large fires were visible on the horizon. A man there said, "That's the airfield."

When I asked, another explained that what we were seeing were barrels of oil being explosively flung into the air and then bursting into flames. We watched till we had to leave for curfew.

Saturday February 3, as I realized the next day, marked thirty-one months in prison camps for my family. As usual, I went for our family rations with our meal tickets. Just as I got behind the Main Building, there was a tremendous sound and yelling as everyone looked up. A pair of American Marine planes (Douglas SBD-6 Dauntless dive bombers) with their canopies opened roared over very, very low.[34] (Nine dive bombers according to the official 1st Cavalry history, but I only saw two.) I could see the pilot's face of the closer plane and saw him throw something out of the cockpit. Then they were gone, and I could go to get our rations.

Before I was back to the shack, the word was all over the camp that he had thrown out his goggles with a note, "Roll out the barrel. Your Christmas will be today or tomorrow!" Interestingly, every published

83

version I have seen quotes the note differently, none like the above. But this is what our family heard.

Distant explosions continued to be heard all day. At curfew, we were in our shanty, and not long afterward, as dusk was descending, we heard a terrific roar outside the camp. Camp leaders later wrote that they feared the sound was the Japanese—who they believed planned to execute all men eighteen to fifty years of age (on January 25, the Japanese commandant had the camp make such a list)—coming to start killing.

Then my curiosity nearly killed me. The noise prompted me to step out our back door to run across the shantytown to the shack of the family of the girl my age with red hair from the Happy Life Blues. From there, I'd be able to see what was going on at the gate. Our shack's back door is seen in figure 16.1, along with my sister and a little neighbor boy.

Figure 16.1. The back of our shack in a photo taken shortly after February 3, 1945. I crouched on the walk just in front of where the small neighbor boy sits next to Babs.

I hadn't noticed a guard standing at the end of the path by the front of our shack just fifteen feet away. He barked something, and I spun around, freezing in a crouch as he put his gun to his shoulder. I looked down the wrong end of the barrel. The gun was just like the one Dad had carved as a toy for my brother, but this was real.

I don't know how long our frozen tableau lasted. I didn't breath and had no idea what to think or do. He had his bayonet on the rifle, standard for the guards. The tableau froze—a skinny ten-and-a-half-year-old kid of fifty-one pounds and a guard, who probably weighed not much more than twice that. He was dressed in his uniform with puttees and a soft cap with a flap hanging down behind, an image burned in my memory. We were equally unsure of the sounds.

Finally he apparently decided that I was no threat and lowered his gun. I made a leap to my right, landing hard on my right shoulder just inside the shack. My parents said nothing. That Japanese soldier would die within the month in the Battle for Manila. My thanks to his memory.

The Great Evening of February 3

Back in the shack, we waited. Then we heard a loud rumbling noise around our camp. The noise stopped at the front gate, and there were explosions and small arms gunfire and a lot of yelling. Then it moved into camp.

We looked out and, seeing no Japanese guards, our family cautiously ventured out in front of our shanty, peering through the gathering dusk down the road toward the Main Building. My siblings and I squatted Filipino fashion next to my standing parents.

Figure 16.2. Our family stood on the road just in front of the faint gray square where our air raid shelter was, across from and just beyond the right end of the Education Building.

Suddenly, in a heart-stopping rush of excitement, we saw an *American Soldier*!

He loped down the road, huge and strange, wearing a strange uniform with a strange helmet and carrying a funny little gun (M1 carbine) and a little metal box (walkie-talkie). His boots were the biggest I had ever seen. He was a free American soldier, and he had come for us!

He asked Dad if there were "any Japs around," and Dad said something and pointed to their barracks on the lower floors of the Education Building.

The soldier said something about "perimeter" and kept going toward the hospital and the wall there. We didn't know that there were only a hundred American soldiers versus sixty-seven Japanese guards, in a city that we thought had twenty thousand Japanese (actually seventeen thousand Japanese marines and soldiers).

The Americans had come a hundred miles through Japanese-held territory to reach us.[35] The Flying Column of 700 men had set off on January 31 from just west of the town of Cabanatuan, not far from the Cabanatuan prison camp, depicted in the movie of their rescue on January 30. The front of the column got through before the enemy blew a bridge over the Tuliahan River during the night of the second, leaving the forty-mile-long remainder of the column stranded temporarily and our saviors isolated.

It got quiet as we stood or squatted on the road in front of our shack. Then we could see tanks and more soldiers coming up the road. They got to the Education Building, and an internee inside called out, "There are Japs on the first two floors, as well as fellow prisoners on the third."

Other voices were calling out, telling where the guards were in the building.

I watched the lead tank turn and drive right up the front door of the building, poking his big gun into the lobby. In a flash, the guards broke down the suwali hall dividers, making hostages of the 226 prisoners there. Our soldiers were exchanging gunfire with guards in the building, and another tank came up. My sister remembered them taking down our shack's nipa front window covering to put it under a machine gun in our front yard. It was one of four machine guns that covered the four sides and roof of the Education Building.

About this time, the American soldiers motioned us back, and a few minutes later, an American lieutenant was shot in the hand while sitting in his jeep in front of our shack. Dad herded us into our air-raid shelter. Mom ducked out and brought back our last hoarded food reserve, a beautiful twelve-ounce can of Argentinian corned beef!

I opened the can with its key and was given the top of the can to lick out, to get every last little bit of fat and suet. We passed the can around with a spoon, each taking a tiny bite and savoring it slowly like ambrosia. And indeed, in our starving condition, it was far better, with protein, fat, and wonderful calories.

No memory of a meal compares to that first meal as free people when, just an hour before, we were starving captives whose leaders feared our massacre. We ate the whole can slowly and in tiny bits in one sitting, not spread out over several days as we usually did. We divided it equally, and since I had the lid, the rest of the family used fingers and tongues to extract every last bit of fat sticking to the main part of the can. Washing the can would not have made it much cleaner. But we were full!

We had survived starvation! Both Mom and Dad were large-boned people, but he was down to 134 pounds, and a good part of that was the accumulated water from his beriberi swollen legs. Mom, at 96 pounds, was lighter than she had been as a teenager. But my weight and that of my siblings must be compared with that of our parents. We children were well fed by comparison. Things quieted down and we left the shelter and went to bed in our shack there on the American front line across from the guards in the Education Building.

To this day, I celebrate the Third of February.

CHAPTER 17
FIRST DAYS OF FREEDOM

As soon as I awoke in the loft of our shack the next morning, I remembered we were free! We peered at the Education Building, but little was happening. Our first problem was food, and the soldiers gave us some from the few K-rations they still had. A soldier gave me a delicious little tin of a cheese/butter combination from his K-ration that I shared in little bites. It was almost as good as the corned beef. Then I was given a little wrapped cube of chocolate. We had not had any chocolate in years, but it was very bitter and I really didn't like it. Soldiers told us that they were intended to be emergency rations and deliberately made less tasty so that it would be the last thing eaten.

Since the soldiers were short of cigarettes, Dad gave them the one pack he had been saving. They were as dry as dust, and the soldiers were not impressed, but apparently any cigarettes were better than none.

That day, I watched as some men who were hostages in the Education Building made ropes of sheets and slid down to the ground. I saw one so weak he collapsed halfway down, fell, and couldn't move. Two GIs shouldered their guns and ran zigzag to the edge of the building, picked him up like the lightweight scarecrow he was, and carried him back to safety. The hostage prisoners at the windows of the Education

Building are seen in figure 17.1. Japanese soldiers kept well away from the windows.

Shooting eased off, and a truce was arranged, in which food for the Education Building was provided for both guards and hostages, who ate after the Japanese soldiers had had their fill.

We talked to GIs (a word I had just learned) near our shack and learned they were from the 1st Cavalry. I also discovered that they would lie down and sleep anywhere and at every opportunity and were frequently asleep when we children came to visit.

Figure 17.1 Photo of hostages in the Education Building from *Life* magazine.

Now, whenever cavalry rides to the rescue in a movie, I think of those brave men who came in on what could have been, and perhaps should have been, a suicide mission. Thank goodness they achieved surprise, or the 67 guards in the concrete Education Building could have made a real fight. We were equally fortunate that the Japanese did not send a contingent from their nearby main force to wipe us out.

With a bridge over the Tuliahan River blown, only 200 of the Flying Column initially entered Manila. The 100 GIs at Santo Tomas had to surround guards in the Education Building, man the perimeter of the camp, and work with the elected camp officials to assure the feeding of 3,700 starving prisoners. Eventually, more of the 700 men of the Flying Squadron reached Manila. All this time, we were cut off, with supplies of food and ammunition a hundred miles away, and our troops had useless, weak former prisoners to defend.

It took several days before the rest of the American Army advanced and supplies could get through. With full access to the former Japanese storeroom (bodega), the camp ate well, even if our food selection did not change. However, the GIs could not stomach the lugao that we relished and went hungry. I felt sorry for them but could not understand their reluctance to eat what we did.

Mom was quite concerned that we could badly hurt ourselves overeating, so for a few days, she limited us to three tablespoons of lugao every few hours. Some internees were so starved that their stomachs had atrophied. Since they did not eat in small quantities, their stomachs could not accommodate that much food, and several died from overeating. Sixty-five more were so wasted away that even food, proper medicine, and hospital care could not save them. But we gained a pound a day.

Shortly after liberation, we discovered there were Japanese prisoners in the basement of the Main Building. Having bowed to them for so long, this was too good to pass up. They were in a cage with bars, and we stared at them like animals in a zoo. Their American guard told us that they were the first prisoners that the 1st Cavalry had taken since the beginning of the war and that they had taken them only because there were women and children around.

Later, I would learn of Japanese false surrenders so as to make suicide hand grenade attacks on their captors and of their code of no surrender. That, and atrocities committed on captured American soldiers, left little belief in the fact that they were really surrendering.

Their American guard told us kids they had found a paper in the commandant's office indicating that we were scheduled to be killed the morning after we were liberated, on February 4. I have not found this reported elsewhere, but this could have been a copy of the order to kill us if rescue appeared eminent.

In his 1971 book, *Japan's Imperial Conspiracy*, David Bergamini, then a civilian prisoner of fifteen at Bilibid five hundred yards from Santo Tomas states on page xxiv that they were told by departing guards that Bilibid Camp execution was scheduled for February 5, the day the 1st Cavalry and the 37th Ohio stumbled upon and liberated them.[36]

The Flying Column

MacArthur had been highly concerned about a possible massacre, and in his view, the advance down Luzon from the landing at Lingayen on the northwest coast was going too slowly. We were too many, too weak, and too deep in Japanese-held territory to be taken to safety. He ordered General Mudge to have a 1st Cavalry Flying Column (actually four such were formed) to punch through and the 37th Ohio Division to attack down to their west to provide flank support.[37]

The Second Flying Column left at one minute before midnight of February 1, coming through a hole made by successive blows by the First Flying Column. It was told to avoid firefights and to bounce off and go around. They were supported by Marine Air groups 32 and 24, who kept nine Douglas SBD-6 Dauntless dive bombers over the column during daylight hours, controlled from a vehicle in which Brigadier General William C. Chase, the US general riding with the column, frequently rode.[38] They started with 700 troops, their key element Company B of the 44th Tank Battalion.[39]

The Flying Column left from just west of Cabanatuan, northwest of where US Rangers, Alamo Scouts, guerrillas, a P-61 Army Air Corp airplane, and Filipino civilians had, on January 30, rescued and evacuated 511 US military prisoners in the first rescue raid. The planes we saw on February 3 were their Marine support fighters. I heard stories of the Flying Column finding Japanese soldiers in their G strings out farming, who just waved to them and of encountering resistance and going around if the Marine fighter planes could not handle the problem quickly.

Occasionally, they found stiff resistance, and many acts of heroism were needed to get them through to us. Filipino soldiers from the vast network of Filipino-American guerillas helped guide them.

The hundred-man part of the column spearheaded by the Third Tank Platoon under Robert E. Lee, Jr., a descendant of the Confederacy's greatest general, headed for Santo Tomas, while others went to capture other key points in the city. Arriving at the camp, they circled part of it, the noise we heard, and then broke down the gate. The column lost people in the lead jeep to a Japanese hand grenade and killed the camp's highly unpopular Japanese lieutenant, who attacked the column with his samurai sword and a hand grenade. As we watched, they then moved to corral the Japanese guards in the Education Building. Others took over the rest of the camp, and the camp's wall became their perimeter.

Joseph C. Huber Jr.

Bilibid Rescue

Bilibid was a penitentiary that had been scheduled for demolition in 1940. It was of an old American plan of buildings, fanning out from a central core like spokes on a wheel. It was used by the Kempeitai for brutal interrogations and was the home to soldiers made to slave on the Manila docks. At the end, it was a military hospital for the remaining 828 soldiers. On Christmas Eve 1944, 447 prisoners from the civilian camp at Baguio were brought there in advance of the American invasion at Lingayan Gulf.

On the fourth, soldiers of the First Cav and leading elements of the Ohio 37th Division stumbled upon old Bilibid Prison, three long blocks from Santo Tomas.[40] Before they arrived, their guards had told the prisoners they were leaving (apparently to join the main force).

Prisoners heard military noises outside the camp and thought the Japanese were coming back—until they heard American voices. The soldiers were concerned that the prison held Japanese soldiers—until they heard American voices and forced the gate.

One teenage boy tells of riding a tank and giving it directions in the town he knew well. All prisoners had to be moved temporarily, as fighting became too intense near Bilibid, but were soon returned, except for one woman brought to Santo Tomas to have a baby. On their return, they found the camp stripped by city neighbors, who had sheltered in the camp during the shelling. It was terrible to lose everything left behind when one had so little. But that was the case for the Filipino civilians as well.

The War's Strangest Scene

On the third day, an agreement was reached between the American colonel and the colonel of the guards in the Education Building, in which our former guards marched out under their flag with a weapon apiece. They were escorted by columns of our troops on each side to a point a mile (or five blocks, according to another account) away; from there, they were to continue on, and our 1st Cavalry detachment would return to camp.[41] This was the only time in the war that armed Japanese and American soldiers marched together.

At last, we were free from the fear of shooting from the guards in the Education Building. We no longer had to go roundabout through the shantytowns to the bathrooms.

A soldier came back from escorting the guards and told my parents that the Japanese wanted to be escorted farther and farther, but the American officer in charge refused to take them past Laguaria Street. This soldier said that the Filipino guerrillas were waiting in the next block for the Japanese. It seems unlikely, but the Japanese soldiers were concerned about going into city streets with irate and noisy civilians and did not want to proceed.[42]

Real Freedom

Nervous energy kept me going after our former guards marched out. I found a piece of a belt of machine gun ammunition with five live bullets, which Dad would not let me keep. I ran with it to the field at the front of the camp where the American Army had set up their big guns—105 mm as I learned from a soldier there—to fire on the Japanese who were then defending the center of Manila. Soldiers there sent me running to a machine gun at the hospital gate near our shack.

Joseph C. Huber Jr.

There, I learned the gun was a water-cooled .30 caliber and, through my inquisitiveness, a lot about that machine gun, squatting Filipino fashion beside the gun and soldiers. For all that, though, the GI said that the belt was of not much use, but he agreed to take it.

Ahead was the deadly Battle of Manila.

CHAPTER 18

THE FIRST RESCUE: CABANATUAN

Much later, we learned about the prisoner rescue which started the series of rescues. While we were starving, the guards at the military prison camp northeast of Cabanatuan on the main Japanese withdrawal road had marched away on January 6. The prisoners there were 511 survivors of Bataan and Corregidor, considered too weak or ill to be worth sending to one of Japan's slave labor camps outside the Philippines. The last such shipment of slave labor had been in December.

The guards leaving meant that the inmates could break into Japanese food stocks and even leave the camp to catch and butcher two carabaos. They were not really left alone, as days later, passing Japanese convoys began bivouacking there, using the camp guards' barracks. But they had food! And the soldiers stopping there overnight were not their guards.

Then, on January 26, George Lapham, one of Luzon's more successful guerrilla leaders of those who had not surrendered after Corregidor fell, rode a mule into the US lines. He informed the US command of the existence of the camp called the Military Cabanatuan Prison Camp and argued that the soldiers there were liable to be massacred.

It is not known whether the local US commanders were aware of the August 1944 Japanese order to massacre all prisoners about to be freed or that this had already happened to prisoners on the western Philippine island of Palawan. But whether this was known or just that there was concern for these ghosts of Bataan and Corregidor, the colonel immediately took this information to General Kreuger, who just as quickly approved a rescue raid.

The next day, the twenty-seventh, an ad hoc force was assembled—with a Ranger group in command, supported by Alamo Scouts, two guerrilla forces, and a P-61 twin-tailed Black Widow night fighter. Their plan was to penetrate twenty miles behind enemy lines in a march totaling thirty miles, kill the Japanese at the prison, and extract the prisoners. The guerrilla forces were to set up and defend blocking positions on the main road past the camp to hold off the thousands of front-line Japanese troops retreating into the hills. It would be the largest rescue extraction of American prisoners in history, just as the fall of Bataan had been the largest surrender since the surrender of Union soldiers at Harper's Ferry in 1862.

On January 29, Filipino civilian volunteers were added to the mission by the raiding force. Arriving at the prison compound on the evening of the thirtieth and using the buzzing P-61 to distract the Japanese while the small force crossed the final open area, they reached the gate and started the rescue at 7:45 p.m.

Killing an estimated 250 enemy soldiers bivouacked there, they brought the former prisoners out on carabao carts supplied by and driven by volunteer villagers. As they continued their withdrawal with the sick, starving ex-prisoners, other villages provided more and more carabao-drawn carts and drivers. The rescue depended on the success of the guerrilla blocking forces, one of which took heavy casualties but managed to keep the road blocked until all had left the camp. At one point, they had to blow up a bridge. An enemy motorized convoy on the main road that threatened to run into the slow moving column of carts was spotted and wiped out by the P-61. The next morning, January 31, all reached American lines, which had advanced to cut in half the distance they needed to move.

CHAPTER 19

SURVIVING THE FEBRUARY 1945 BATTLE OF MANILA

We former prisoners were fortunate that Admiral Iwabuci had chosen to make his stand in the old walled city (the Intramuros) and in the nearby modern city area with the post office, stadium, and many large buildings. It was 2,200 yards away, so our camp was reasonably safe from small arms, though well within artillery range. Since the Americans had few places for their artillery, their 105mm guns were in the open area in the front of Santo Tomas, and their mortars were behind us.

While the Japanese had plenty of space in the Intramuros for their artillery, American control of the air meant they could not safely place them in the open. As GIs told my parents while we attentively listened, the Japanese hauled their guns up to the upper floors of modern concrete buildings such as the Post Office. There, they would fire a few rounds, pull back while our artillery plastered the building, and then fire again from a different room.

After the Japanese marched out, intense shelling of the camp by the Japanese began, being most intense on the fifth through the seventh. During the worst of the nighttime shelling, we went behind the Education Building to sleep on cots in the open. I would lie there looking up at tracers overhead and shells, probably mortars, whomping and arching up toward the Japanese. I remember thinking as I fell asleep that I must remember this because it was important. Fortunately, it did not rain.

One of those nights, Dad was too sick to come with us, and Mom told us kids to stay behind the Education Building, while she went back while we were being shelled to help Dad. We were asleep before Mom returned after finding a military doctor, who went to see him in our shack. Next morning, we went back to the shack and found that a shell had landed some forty yards away from it. Fortunately, it was a dud. We kids squatted around it and could clearly see its base sticking up above the hard ground. If there had been another shell in the series it would have struck our shack—and Dad.

In all, seventeen of us recently freed internees were killed.[43] A man I knew was killed when a shell hit their room on the third floor of the Main Building. One was killed when a shell hit the Education Building across from our shack. Fifteen GIs and eight Filipinos were also killed, and a number were wounded in our camp compound. Including those wounded, we suffered a casualty rate of over 3 percent, 5 percent if those who died of the effects of starvation after liberation are included.[44] However, walking around in the daytime was safe, as the Japanese guns were quiet during the day, when it was not safe for them to fire.

We began to recover from starvation. In the first month, after liberation I went from fifty-one pounds to eighty-one and was still skinny. Most were gaining a pound a day. Our weight loss is perhaps best seen in figure 19.1, a photograph taken during the Battle of Manila.

On the seventh, MacArthur spent a very few minutes in the camp. But by the time I learned of his appearance and rushed over, he had left.

Joseph C. Huber Jr.

I never got to see this man, whose decisions had saved our lives many times, with an ego unmatched even by Nero and Hitler. In all the war, I never met a GI with a positive attitude toward him, and my own feelings are very mixed. Before and at the beginning of the war, he blundered terribly, yet his vision of the primacy of the Philippines and for the urgent rescue of the Allied prisoners meant 7,700 prisoners survived! I did get to hear Osmania, the president of the Philippines. Boring.

A military hospital was set up on the lower two floors of the Education Building across from our shack. It was farthest from the nearest Japanese guns and, with the Japanese guards gone, empty. I remember seeing piles of bloody bandages as I walked past the end of the building, going between our shack and the latrines and showers behind the education building. A kid said he had seen part of a leg on a pile there, but despite looking hard, I never saw any body part.

Figure 19.1 Our family shortly after liberation—(from left to right) Stephen, Dad, Barbara, Mom, and myself.

After we were no longer cut off in the Japanese-held city, and supplies could finally came in, there were all sorts of nourishing canned goodies for our meals. We particularly loved Spam. Through some logistics quirk, the only fruit was canned apricots. It wasn't bad. But, as it was the only fruit, my family built up a dislike for the taste of apricots that is with me today.

We had real bread, though, and when I got our family rations, there were ten slices for the five of us. I gloried in it until a starving Filipino driving a callesa, a light two-wheeled, covered passenger cart drawn by a horse and used as a taxi, asked for food for his family.

I was torn. The food I had was for my family, who had gone through starvation, sharing food in exact, even portions. Yet I felt his hunger. After dithering, I finally broke a piece of bread in half and gave it to him. The shame that I did not give more I will carry to my grave.

Shortly after liberation, the 1st Cavalry pulled out to fight elsewhere and the 37th Ohio Division took over our camp.[45] Mom and Dad, being Ohioans, became the focus of visits, with cigarettes and gifts. The GIs longed to talk to civilians from home, and when not on the line, they would walk the mile or so back to our camp to relax with Ohio civilians. Most importantly, they brought news. I stuck very close to hear every bit of the blow-by-blow descriptions of the Battle of Manila, which the visiting GIs were witnessing daily.

Of these many reports, the most vivid was the attack on the Intramuros, with its forty-foot-thick stone and earthen walls. Visitors told of pushing pipes filled with explosives (bangalore torpedoes) into a hole created by a tank shell and detonating it. Tanks were used to push strings of such pipes to be detonated to enlarge the opening. This was repeated until a hole was blasted clear through, allowing entrance into the old fort.

Others told of trying to destroy the illusive Japanese artillery guns in modern buildings. A gun would be spotted firing out a window, and a barrage would be laid to try to take out the gun before it fired a few rounds and was moved. Faces of many buildings were smashed in.

Another told of the parachute attack on Corregidor, with its appalling number of injuries from falling on the rough, rocky terrain in the middle of Manila harbor. He said that one in four parachutists was injured by the rough terrain.

What they did not speak of were the ghastly stories of the Japanese massacres of civilians in Manila during the battle. Troops came back to visit because it offered a place of normalcy and tranquility, with families and children from their home state. No word of the horror was expressed.

About a week after liberation, my sister and I were hanging about a few tanks in front of the Main Building. They had vivid names like Battling Basic, the tank that led the force and broke down the gate, Bouncing Beulah, and Georgia Peach. We wanted to climb on them, and when we asked a soldier if we could, he asked us to sit on the gun for a picture. I sat in front with Babs behind me. We looked for Steve but could not see him, so another boy sat behind Babs. They gave me a cartridge belt (see figure 19.2) and a pair of binoculars to hold. Then another soldier (probably a war correspondent) took a few pictures and said it would be in the papers. I said, "Sure!" and got down and handed back the "props." But indeed, the image appeared on the top of the front page of the *Akron Beacon Journal*.

Figure 19.2. Copy of the February 16, 1945, *Akron Beacon Journal*.

Since the caption mentioned our brother Steve and said nothing about our parents, our American relatives could assume the whole family had survived. The paper contacted our family and found it was the first news since a letter dated June 25, 1943, when we were still at the Happy Life Blues Camp.

The Battle of Manila raged for a bloody month. Besides a number of newly liberated internees killed by shells, 1,010 American servicemen lost their lives, as did the 16,665 Japanese marines and army soldiers. That included Admiral Iwabuci, who apparently committed suicide, as did many Japanese soldiers.

Most horrifying, though, were the deaths of over 100,000 Filipinos. Many were massacred by the Japanese, some in sight of American soldiers on the other side of the Pasig River, unable to interfere. As the Japanese fought to the last man, it was finally necessary to use larger weapons than MacArthur had originally allowed in order to minimize the loss of American soldiers.[46] All told, some 120,000 people lost their lives between that glorious third of February and the third of March, when the battle was officially declared over.

The sixty-four military nurses from Bataan, Corregidor, and Manila were trucked out almost immediately, the first to return home. They had survived Bataan or Corregidor and Santo Tomas. These included the ten who had been with us at the Davao "convent" camp.

Only in later years did I come to appreciate the awful cost in lives of our survival. For each of us, some ten Filipinos were massacred in direct retaliation for rescue raids or in massacres. Counting the total of US, Filipino, and Japanese deaths in the liberation of the Philippines, sixty people died for each rescued prisoner, a terrible price.

CHAPTER 20
LOS BAÑOS RESCUE

Between January 30 and the February 4, hastily formed ad hoc groups had rescued the 511 at Cabanatuan, the 3,768 of us at Santo Tomas, and the 1,275 at the old Bilibid Penitentiary Prison. Guerrillas, Filipino civilians, US Army commands, Marine Air, Rangers, Alamo Scouts, and a Tank Battalion of US cavalry had participated. However, there were still 2,147 Allied prisoners at Los Baños, located some sixty miles south in the midst of the crack Japanese 8th Division defending the southern approaches to Manila. They were in a camp two and a half miles from the south end of Lake Laguna de Bay and included ten Navy nurses.[47]

The US 11th Airborne, who had been fighting their way from their southern landing, was given the task of saving the Los Baños prisoners.[48] They had begun gathering data about the time of the Santo Tomas rescue. Using information from two escapees from Los Baños, a two-man scouting foray, and Filipino/American guerrillas, a detailed appreciation of the camp, its Japanese defenders, and the Japanese 8th Division forces was obtained. Then General MacArthur visited Division Commander General Swing and ordered the raid.

Beginning on February 18, forces to be used were pulled out from the line where they were fighting pillbox-by-pillbox and told of their new assignment. On the February 19, an extremely complicated plan was developed. This involved a parachute drop from a hastily gathered group of C-47s flying from Leyte via newly retaken Nichols Air Field to be secured by infiltrating Filipino guerrillas and a land attack to open an escape route. A waterborne force was to cross Lake Laguna de Bay, and guerrillas were to secure the beachhead for the waterborne force. Another team was to penetrate the camp stealthily on foot to kill the guards. Units involved were the 127th Airborne Engineering, a guerrilla unit, the 11th Airborne, the 511th and 188th Parachute Infantry Regimental Combat Teams, and the 672nd Amphibious Tractor Battalion.

The commander of the selected company led the effort, though he was outranked by others involved. The waterborne force was accompanied by a major general on MacArthur's staff, bent on scooping up Japanese documents. H hour was 0706 five days later on the twenty-third.

Initial success was achieved! However, it became apparent that the force tasked with clearing a land evacuation route could not get through in time, if at all. The company commander changed the plan and ordered a total evacuation by water. He had to burn the camp down in order to get the confused ex-prisoners, who wanted to take everything (a natural instinct developed from years of deprivation in prison) to move to the waiting Alligators, LVT (4)s (an amphibious tracked vehicle capable of running on land with propellers for in-water use, normally mounting a machine gun and capable of carrying a number of people or a large amount of supplies).

Despite some casualties and the need to make multiple trips, the evacuation was successful, leaving the guerrillas to exit as they had come. The last LVTs leaving were fired upon and returned fire. The 11th Division Commander General Swing flew overhead and communicated with the ground commander, inquiring as to the ability of retaining a beachhead at the lake landing site. Wisely, the commander executed a "Nelson blind-eye to the signal flags" by pretending that radio contact had been broken.

Following the success of what was now the largest rescue and evacuation of Allied prisoners, many claimed credit. The company commander was ordered to prepare predated orders, so that it would not be evident that there was no written plan and that the operation had actually been done on the fly, like a pickup football play.

CHAPTER 21
SUMMARY

In twenty-four days, over 7,700 weak starving prisoners had been rescued, 2,658 extracted from behind enemy lines in an effort that took only twenty-nine days, including preparation! Keys to success were local command with a defined mission, and luck, which mostly resulted from audacity and resourcefulness. No rescue had more than five days to prepare, and security was outstanding. Despite a paucity of formal paperwork, no logistics failures occurred. Plans were changed on the spot as needed, without recourse to high authority—a far cry from the top-level direction of more recent failed rescue efforts.

But the diversity of forces is, perhaps, the most amazing thing. These included five different guerrilla forces, civilians from a village, air support from four different army and marine air groups, seven different army organizations, and three generals who rode or flew overhead but did not try to exercise local command in the operations. Equally amazing was the level of cooperation, coordination, and support!

CHAPTER 22
GOING HOME

As February drew to a close, the American Army destroyed the last Japanese artillery, and fighting was reduced to small arms engagements, following nearly point-blank artillery attacks on buildings, too distant to impinge on Santo Tomas. The city was officially declared free on February 27, and the battle was officially over on March 3, a full month after it started.

On March 13, 1945, we got our orders (see figure 22.1). We gathered our meager possessions and, without regret, turned our back on the shack that had been home for a year, just as we had left the shanty we'd built at Happy Life Blues.

As we stood or sat in the open truck, we were shocked at the state of the City of Manila. The buildings in camp were essentially intact. But in the rest of the city, building after building had only one or two walls remaining, and floors hung down from a single wall like curtains. Everything was covered in dust, and there were piles of dirt and rubble everywhere. Streets were pockmarked with holes and obstructed with brick and concrete debris, through which our trucks picked their way. Many large buildings had their whole fronts smashed in. Manila was destroyed like Warsaw, the two worst in World War II.

Years later, I thought of those survivors for whom that rubble was home. On the July 4, 1945, the Philippines were declared an independent nation. On July 14, Santo Tomas Internment Camp was closed, with the remaining prisoners moved to another camp to await further moves. The campus became a major US Military hospital, probably in anticipation of the invasion of Japan. Many had made the Philippines their home and had real difficulty in finding transportation.

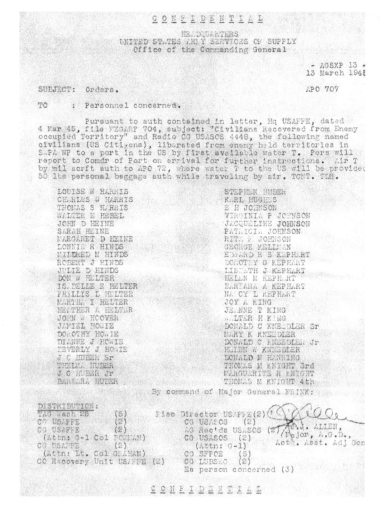

Figure 22.1. Our orders home.

But we were lucky. We had a company, Goodyear, and a home in Akron, Ohio. Those staying behind had a devastated economy and were also suffering the effects of imprisonment.

On March 13, we arrived at Clark Field. We saw many wrecked Japanese planes pushed off the runway at crazy angles and many large holes in the runway and taxiways. We went to sit on the floor of a damaged hangar out of the sun. We waited and stared out at the holes in the door and in the roof. We got K-rations and water and waited.

Finally, we were told we would not go that day and piled back into trucks and rode back to Santo Tomas, paying little attention to anything. We spent the night in our old beds in the shanty. The next morning, we again left early, and, while aware of the city, we had seen it.

This time we promptly boarded a twin-engine C-47 (DC-3) and climbed the steep slope of the cabin. We were shown to shallow bucket seats on the side of the plane facing inwards and told how to buckle a seat belt, a real novelty. Our family was on the right-hand side of the plane, about a third of the way from the back. In the center of the cabin, running the length of the passenger compartment, was a tied-down pile of stuff.

We had been given Mae West life jackets and instructed on how to inflate them if we got in the water. Even uninflated, they were bulky enough on our skinny frames that it made it hard to twist around to see out of the plane's windows behind us. After we got up in the air and were allowed to unbuckle our seat belts, we discovered there were better places to look out. Cracks in the floor and on the side of the plane let us see the ground below and out the sides of the aircraft. We children were asked if we would like to see the cockpit, and when I asked about the little black baby clouds that we saw appearing suddenly, the pilot said that that was Japanese antiaircraft guns shooting at us, but not to worry.

We landed at Tacloban on Leyte, ending my first airplane ride. Here, they made all the men get into separate trucks from the women and children. When the folks asked why, it was because the men were to go to a separate "recuperation" camp. Mom was really upset! The American Army had done what the Japanese Army had failed to do throughout our imprisonment—separate the family!

After what seemed like a long drive, we were put in a tent with a number of cots with other women and children. We learned the routine of chow line, and there was lots of food. Dad soon hitchhiked to visit but was not allowed to stay overnight. We started on Atabrin, causing our skin to turn yellow to match the soldiers.

There were movies on nights it didn't rain, projected on a sheet stretched between coconut trees, with benches made from split trees. Every morning, recovering soldiers or nearby sailors would come to ask Mom if we children could come out and play, and we would be out all day, giving Mom a chance to relax.

The camp was on the ocean, so we went swimming. One day, they got an inflated raft, and we went out into the surf. The up and down in the waves was a lot of fun—that is, until the raft turned over, and I ended up on the bottom of the ocean, swallowing what seemed like an enormous amount of salty seawater. That sensation of drowning I do not wish to repeat. Once rescued, I sat with a couple of soldiers on the sand trying to get my breath back and waiting for my head to feel right again. I declined going on the raft again.

To the soldiers, we were the first American children they had seen in some time. I think we represented a taste of home, of normal life. And of course, they knew looking at us that we had been through starvation. We were the recipients of all the care, food, and attention they could give us. Since they were convalescing, they had lots of time on their hands.

One time, a bunch of us kids were taken in jeeps to a strange-looking building, a Quonset hut. Here, we sat at real tables and chairs and were given cake and something white in a bowl. I'm afraid that the three Huber children were not good guests. We loved the cake, the first in almost three years. But we had no idea what this hard, cold, yucky stuff in the bowl was. It was rock hard, cold, and not something any civilized person would want to put in their mouth. We picked away at it and finally declined the rest. I'm sure our hosts couldn't imagine red-blooded American children turning down good vanilla ice cream.

Then we gathered around a soldier sitting outside, who had an oversized doll on his lap. He was a ventriloquist and entertained us for some time as the dummy talked to each of us in turn and told jokes (see figure 22.2).

After several days, we took trucks to a dock and boarded a Landing Craft Personnel. At the last minute, Dad showed up, and we went out to a ship and climbed up a stairway on the side. It was the S.S. *Klipfontein*, a converted Dutch cargo ship that normally carried a few passengers. Women and children civilians, 143 in total, were in its few former passenger cabins, which had been converted into dormitories with four- and five-high stacks of bunks made of canvas on pipe frames. You had to crawl into them. Men bunked with the soldiers.

We had two meals a day in the dining room, and Mom took bread and stuff in a napkin to make a lunch. We wandered around the deck loaded with wounded soldiers, some missing limbs and many on crutches and wearing bandages. None would talk about their experiences in the war or how they had been injured. Nor would any answer my first question, "Did you kill any Japs?" At age ten, the latter seemed like a logical question.

Figure 22.2. Us children talking to the ventriloquist dummy. My brother, Steve, is the blond on the right. Barbara is half hidden behind him and me, the closest to the dummy, wearing an army cap.

But they would talk about MacArthur, not nicely. I vividly remember bitter comments about his sending troops into Guadalcanal (wherever that was) armed with .30-03 Springfields. They said they should have had tommy guns and carbines for jungle fighting. One soldier said MacArthur's behavior was criminal.

They were, on the other hand, more curious about where we were from and about our experiences. And I'm afraid I talked a lot. In retrospect, perhaps that wasn't such a bad idea, although I am not sure that my defense of MacArthur for saving our lives was particularly appreciated. We thought the food was wonderful, but I heard many complaints from the soldiers about the food and the terrible crowding

RESCUE RAIDS OF LUZON!

in the holds converted to vast dormitories of multistacked pipe-and-canvas bunks.

From Tacloban, Leyte, we sailed south to the island of Biak off the northwest coast of New Guinea. Our route took us across the equator, and we watched a Davy Jones Crossing-the-Equator ceremony (an initiation commemorating one's first crossing of the equator). Men dressed in funny outfits sat in chairs and sentenced the initiates to do funny things, mostly getting dunked in a big pool of water there on the deck.

Our first night at Biak, American antiaircraft guns were firing, and searchlights swept the sky. I looked out the window of our cabin at the ships anchored there and at the arcs of the shells. Japanese planes were making a raid. After its capture in bitter fighting against 11,000 Japanese soldiers (who died or committed suicide rather than surrender), Biak had been turned into an enormous hospital complex.

After stops at Hollandia and Finschaven in New Guinea, to pick up more convalescing soldiers, we headed for the States. Since the *Klipfontein* was a fast cargo ship, it traveled alone from Finschaven, zigzagging across the Pacific. Lifeboat drills were held at dawn (an ugly time to be roused out of bed) and dusk, when there was the greatest threat of Japanese submarines. We put our life jackets on and went to sit on deck beside the lifeboat to which we were assigned. Mornings were best because our station was on the starboard side, and we could watch the sun come up. Each group of us had a couple of sailors to launch and man our lifeboat. Stacks of rafts were lashed to the superstructure for the hundreds of recuperating GIs.

At sunrise on April 13, the PA system announced that President Franklin Delano Roosevelt had died. For us former internees, it was like a hammer blow. At that point, we needed stability. I remember being very concerned and asked Dad what would happen. He said he was sure that things would work out.

The trip of weeks continued—eating, sleeping, talking with soldiers, and watching the waves and the occasional fish or dolphins. We would have liked to run around the deck, but it was so packed with wounded soldiers whose only alternative were their bunks, that careful walking was our exercise. They must have felt it incongruous to have us healthy young kids wandering about. Hopefully, we weren't a nuisance.

One day we were told to pack our meager belongings, as we were soon coming into port. Soon we could see land, and the rails were crowded with soldiers and us civilians. Being small, we children wiggled to the front. Finally, we saw the wonderful sight of San Francisco's answer to the Statue of Liberty, the Golden Gate Bridge, in all its glory on a beautiful sunny morning. Horns sounded on cars as we passed under it, and fireboats with sprays of water accompanied us. We were home!

There was cheering at the dock, which was jammed with people as we landed on the April 21, 1945. Mom's aunt, one of her cousins, and two of her aunt's friends met us at the dock, so very elegantly dressed compared to our cast-off army clothes, as seen in the photo in figure 22.3. They took us to rooms at the Sir Francis Drake Hotel, San Francisco's finest. The grown-ups were talking a mile a minute, and it was good just to listen.

Mom's aunt took us children clothes shopping (some from under the counter when told of our experience). Mom wrote she took a long tub bath, her first since 1940. We thought we were going to stay awhile, but the company had reservations for staterooms on a train leaving that night. If we didn't go then, it wasn't clear when we could get back to Akron.

We didn't know how lucky we were. Every seat was filled, and we ate in shifts. It was wonderful watching out the train windows and eating on white tablecloths with heavy silverware in the dining car, with our whole family eating together again. I saw snow and had to ask my folks to tell me about that white stuff.

Figure 22.3. Homecoming at San Francisco—(from left to right, back row) a friend of Mom's aunt, Mom's aunt, another of her aunt's friends, and a cousin and (from left to right, front row) Mom, Steve, me, Barbara, and Dad.

When we reached Chicago, Dad told us only pigs got to ride through Chicago. People had to get off one train, take a cab across town, and catch another train. The second train took us to Akron, arriving at the old Akron train station under the bridge on East Market Street on April 24, 1945. We looked like refugees in army cast-offs, as seen in the photograph in figure 22.4.

Our family crowded the station, along with a reporter and photographer from the city's newspaper, to greet us. We had been away for almost five years. We eventually got to Akron's premier hotel, the Mayflower, and were ensconced in luxury unimaginable just two months earlier. The photo in figure 22.5 was taken a few days later at the hotel, after we had been outfitted in civilian clothes. Hotel food was a real treat.

Helen Waterhouse, the noted *Akron Beacon Journal*'s columnist, took us under her wing and did a full-page spread in the Sunday Rotogravure of us reading the Sunday funnies and playing, of Dad buying a suit, and of Mom getting a new outfit.

Figure 22.4. Greeted by grandparents (from left to right) Barbara, Grandpa Guy Thompson, Mom, Dad, Steve, Grandma Frances Huber, me, and Grandpa Louis Huber.

I was taken to schools to talk about our experiences for war bond stamp drives. Best remembered were a school for the deaf and hard of hearing and East High School, where older cousins were students. I did interviews and broadcasts over the loudspeaker system and talked to individual classes. Everywhere, they asked the same question—did I still like rice? Always my answer was that I hated lugao but loved nice dry rice.

Our parents had pulled us through, healthy and without physiological problems. Even after many years, the only impact of our experience is that we children are shorter than we otherwise would have been. Thanks to regular measurements by an uncle, we know we would have been taller—my brother by two inches, my sister by three, and me by four or five.

Figure 22.5. Our liberated family (from left to right), Dad, Stephen, Mom, me, and Barbara.

It is clear that our survival was a direct result of the strength, determination, skills, intelligence, foresight, and love of our parents, as well as their willingness to take risks. We never doubted their love, and they acted together on everything.

Men in camp without families did not do so well, and our presence was good for Dad. We ate better food, and with the family working together, we produced more and were better for it.

Our assessment of our parents was supported at a much higher level. Even though they were civilians, MacArthur recognized them by awarding them both the Asiatic-Pacific Campaign Medal *with a battle star*!

The citation from his order number FEXD 200.6, dated April 29, 1945, reads, in part:

"Have by their fortitude and courage, contributed materially to the success of the Philippine Campaign."

By order of General MacArthur

The war cost them many years of their lives. Dad did not reach the age of seventy, and Mom died three years later at age sixty-seven. In their later years, my sister's husband, who had been wounded in the Normandy invasion, collapsed and died shortly after their second child was born. She moved back home, and our parents helped care for her two children while she went back to get a teaching degree to go with her fine arts degree.

CHAPTER 23
OUR WAR LESSONS AND IRONIES

General

We didn't learn to hate Japanese people, despite our treatment and the atrocities their military committed. From the treatment of Japanese soldiers by their officers, it was clear that they had been raised very differently. From the propaganda that appeared in their English language papers, it was clear that they were a manipulated people. I understood this better after I had studied their history, addressed in Appendix 1.

Indoctrination begun in infancy can lead people to believe fervently that death for cause, emperor, or religion is the ultimate best use of one's life and is rewarded in the afterlife. This includes the absurdity of suicidal death such as kamikaze, suicide bombing and suicide in lieu of or after surrender. It can also lead to accepting training to commit atrocities.

I came to understand that Americans must be the best self-organizing people in the world, with a firm belief in democracy. Everyone proved willing to take assigned positions. And people pitched in to create entertainment, education, and religious services. We learned to be brave, to be self-sufficient in finding things to occupy our time, and to get along with others thrown together.

But perhaps most importantly, we learned to keep our heads down and do what we were told. It helped that we were raised to be well behaved.

Ironies

War, the ultimate irony, spawned many more for our family (and, I am sure, many others' odysseys) The US navy was supposed to pick us up at the mouth of the Kabasalan River, in a destroyer, no less. But, or course there were no destroyers to came. Thirty years after the war, an article appeared on the adventures of the Guam supply boat, the USS *Gold Star*.[49] At the outbreak of the war, December 9, 1941 (the day after the war started Asian time), it was at nearby Tambanan to pick up a load of lumber. The *Gold Star* sailed toward Zamboanga, going past our river and, after sailing around for a couple of days, sailed for Australia. Had they and we but known, we could have escaped the war and taken precious rubber seedlings and valuable bales of rubber, far more valuable than their load of lumber.

All of the conditions seemed right for taking to the hills. Jungle-covered mountains were so dense that it was later convincingly claimed that an undiscovered, aboriginal "Tsaday" tribe, had been discovered, a hoax that took years to uncover. The lack of quinine made this risky. But the region north of us on the other side of the hills became a guerrilla stronghold never invaded by the Japanese. There, within months of our capture, guerillas were successfully growing cinchona trees for their quinine-producing bark. Supplies were also being provided by submarine by the Spyron network under Commander Chick Parsons. A secret airfield was sixty miles from the planation. And on the plantation, when the two Japanese left to manage it "disappeared," we could have moved back to our house in just two months.

The Greatest Irony

The greatest irony lay in why we were there. The importance of Dad's job was underscored by the fact that the massive effort undertaken to develop synthetic rubber during the war was begun with the bald statement that "failure to successfully develop synthetic rubber *would* cost us the war."

In our hometown of Akron, Ohio, the intensive drive to develop synthetic rubber was successful, the war-winning innovation more important in winning the war than the atom bomb! While little good was said about the short life of synthetic rubber tires, they helped fill the gap. This development obviated the risks and efforts of our parents but in no way decreased their bravery, sacrifices, or losses.

EPILOGUE

We came home to rationing, which Mom thought a joke, giving away extra sugar. Rent control did not permit us to evict the renters of our house and meant we had to buy a new house. There on the Portage Lakes, Dad taught us to swim. The US government provided compensation for those interned at $26.26 per month of internment for children and $64.64 for adults. Dad said this went to the company as a partial payment for the significant personal debts incurred during the war which Goodyear covered.

With health and weight recovered, in November 1945, Dad and the assistant manager took one of the first boats taking civilians back to restart the plantation. Their job in a shattered Philippine economy was formidable. However, at the direction of the Philippine/American guerilla commander on Mindanao, Gen. (Col.) Fertig, the plantation had managed to produce some thirty-three tons of rubber that were shipped out in May 1945.[50]

Without the prewar launch, the assistant manager, an Annapolis grad, went to Cebu to buy a fifty-foot war-surplus LCM (landing craft, mechanized), which was then converted (see figure E.1).

Mom and we children returned on the first boat taking dependents back to the Philippines, the freighter *General Gordon*. Mom accelerated the Calvert home instruction course to make up for schooling lost in the war. It was so much fun we prodded Mom to cut short the short breaks between school "years," and ended up a year ahead.

Figure E.1. Our postwar modified LCM.

We had the luxury of going barefoot except on trips to Zamboanga. School was done by lunchtime. Then came projects, such as taming our wild monkey, Jocko; barefoot tramps through the jungle; or building projects for me and painting for my sister. We read, listened to the shortwave radio, and learned to play bridge.

At age twelve, I talked Dad into letting me maintain the company arsenal. The Japanese army had broken through a blocking force of Filipino guerrillas in the Battle for Zamboanga and fled to within thirty miles of the plantation. From there they had made trips into the plantation looking for food. Fearing that there might still be Japanese soldiers in the hills beyond the 1,285 who'd surrendered, the company had a dozen Thompson submachine guns, eight US Army carbines, a Japanese rifle, and several .45 automatics locked up in the walk-in office vault. I kept one M1 army carbine and clips of ammunition at the house to scare the iguana that lived at the edge of our lawn away from our chickens and to frighten away huge, noisy fruit bats when fruit ripened on a tree near our house.

New Years' and the Fourth of July, I'd fire a clip into the air in place of fireworks. Once we children (11, 12 and 13) fired a Thompson!

Every three months, we put on tennis shoes to go to town, an overnight trip on the LCM, now with fold-down bunks. For three days, we would spend mornings sightseeing and afternoons watching every old movie in town. We visited the ruined Japanese gun emplacements on the hill overlooking Zamboanga and climbed around the old Spanish Fort. It was a wonderful barefoot two years before we came home in 1948. We kids are shown at the front of the LCM in figure E.2.

We returned on a small Swedish freighter, the *Christer Salen*, stopping for three days at the Del Monte pineapple plantation on northern Mindanao. Here I developed a crush on the plantation manager's redheaded daughter. I knew her from the Happy Life Blues in Davao and from Santo Tomas, where her family's shack was not far from our family's shack. Ah, the pangs of hopeless love when we left knowing I would never see her again. I told myself it was an infatuation but it still hurt.

Figure E.2. Going home. Standing on front of the LCM (from left to right) me (Joe Jr.), Stephen, and Barbara, barefoot except Babs.

At the stop at Del Monte, the ship took on pineapples and heavier-than-water logs, which were lashed to the deck, causing the ship to roll excessively in any kind of sea (see figure E.3). I explored the ship from stem to stern, walking down the propeller shaft to the very end and climbing the ladder back to the aft deck more than once. I had the opportunity to steer and discovered steering in a crossing sea is not easy.

Two years later, she broke in half, and her captain sailed the back half of her backwards to China to get a new, very short bow to sail back to Sweden to replace forward end.

Figure E.3. The *Christer Salen* and the heavier-than-water logs on the forward deck.

Our parents settled us with our Huber grandparents to go to school and returned for another tour of duty on the plantation. Graduating first in a small class of sixty-five, due no doubt to Mom's excellent homeschooling, I went on to earn two degrees from the Massachusetts Institute of Technology. From there, I went into the aerospace industry, developing a number of devices for the Cold War, the War on Drugs, and the War on Terror. I earned six US and two international patents and led a number of projects. My work gave me the opportunity of extensive travel, and I was able to take our whole family to Greece for three months on a contract. After I retired, my wife and I and drove four thousand miles in the UK exploring many areas of the country, returning to a centrally located apartment between trips.

We have been blessed with two boys, five grandchildren, and two lovely daughters-in-law. After retirement, my wife and I formed a corporation, she the CEO, which for ten years provided technical services to my former employer. Active participation continues in Rotary International, Torch International, a WWII Round Table, and our church.

Barbara and Stephen, my younger siblings, moved to New Orleans when our parents returned, and Dad was given the task of setting up and operating a Crude Rubber Import Office.

Barbara earned an art degree from the Sophie Newcomb College of Tulane University. She married a college instructor who had been seriously wounded in Normandy in World War II. He collapsed and died just after their second child was born. Moving home, Barbara took an accelerated program to earn a teaching degree and spent thirty years teaching in the deplorable inner city schools of New Orleans. She married an air traffic controller with three sons from a previous marriage who had served in the postwar army in Europe. She and her husband lost their home in Hurricane Katrina and moved to Baton Rouge. Both have passed away.

Stephen went to LSU in Baton Rouge and then into the Air Force for four years, spending time in Colorado and at a then-secret facility in Alice Springs, Australia. On his return, he finished his undergraduate education at LSU (NO), took a law degree from Loyola, and spent a career with an insurance company, leading the litigation section. His marriage has produced a son and a daughter and, to date, two grandsons and a granddaughter.

Our parents continued to be very socially active after their return, but the war had taken a major toll and led to their early deaths. They assured our survival and our good mental and physical health, at great cost to themselves. They represented real parenthood and are truly mourned. Their memory lives on in their six grandchildren and a dozen great-grandchildren, who would not be alive but for their sacrifices and heroic efforts.

APPENDIX 1
THE WHY OF JAPAN'S ACTIONS IN THEIR GREAT PACIFIC WAR, 1931–1945

The why of the need for the rescues and of our slice of the war required a look at the history of Japan to see what shaped her people and the actions of her military. The Japanese people sincerely believed that the Far East would be better off with Japanese leadership. Priding themselves, with good cause, on their culture, it is ironic then that the Japanese are best known in World War II for brutality, atrocities, and twenty million deaths.

Unlike those of the countries they conquered, Japan's population is uniquely homogeneous. A wave of later immigrants whose descendants populate the islands was so prolific they overwhelmed two prior immigrant groups or drove them into the hills. The dense population permitted by sea and soil required that Japanese society be highly structured and constraining, without space for divergence of peoples and cultures.

Until the early seventeenth century, Japan, like many countries, expanded and created hegemonies when she could, conquering Okinawa and Kyushu in 1609 and challenging China for Korea. This effort was foiled by Korea's navy's cannon-firing ironclads, 250 years before the *Monitor*.

Following the Korean debacle, Japan totally closed its doors to the world in 1635, when it, England, France, and Spain, were the world's most powerful nations – and our Pilgrims were getting started. Without isolation, the Pacific and our West Coast may well have been part of the Japanese empire, clashing with America's Manifest Destiny.

To cleanse the nation of outside influences, the rapidly growing numbers of Christian faithful were butchered or driven underground, and a major attempt was made to suppress the Buddhist religion.

Isolation resulted in stagnation of technology; thought; and, more importantly, moral and political stimulation. Japan fell disastrously behind in innovation, colonies, and national influence, fostering a xenophobic attitude. Commodore Matthew in 1853 found a Japan akin to medieval Europe hundreds of years earlier, with real power held by the Shogun.

The emperor was believed to be descended from the sun goddess through the first emperor, known as Jimmu. In 1872, Jimmu was declared to have ruled, beginning February 11, 660 BC [when Rome was growing.]. This is long before the first century AD date that most archeologists and historians posit. The emperor was supported by three ancient families with specific roles, shoguns were from a fourth. Japan was densely populated (30 million as compared to 31 million in the United States in 1853). According to Shinto (the religion of the emperor and, after the purging, most in Japan), all Japanese were considered descendants of the sun goddess.

Efforts to "open" Japan were bitterly contested by Emperor Komei, who repeatedly ordered the shogun to drive the "barbarians" from Japan. Recognizing the impossibility of the order, Emperor Komei was murdered by the leading families, and his son Meiji (then fifteen) installed as emperor on February 3, 1867. While Meiji supported the imperative of driving out the "barbarians," his advisors convinced him that this required that Japan first become strong and then build a buffer empire. With the German guidance and support (at the time of Bismarck and Germany's drive for growth), it set out to create a nation in arms.

A Prussian-style constitution was written giving the emperor the real power, ruling through key nobles, who took the blame for failed policies. The executive was left to two parties, who shared both the common program of national expansion and high levels of corruption.

In less than two generations, Japan metamorphosed into a nearly modern state capable of meeting modern armies on the battlefield. However, it was too late to achieve exclusion of foreigners by expansion, and there were no unclaimed worthwhile territories. But by 1890, Japan was prepared to expand. First came Korea. Then the Sino-Japanese War of 1894–1895, with its atrocities at Port Arthur in Manchuria, with most gains lost in the peace treaties. The seventy thousand white-uniformed soldiers in the 1900 Boxer Rebellion achieved widespread world acclaim for their professionalism, humanity, and fighting ability in supporting European and American forces.

In 1904, Japan provoked the Russo-Japanese War, the first twentieth-century war between major nations. Their German-inspired massed charges proved costly, as they did in World War II. They ended with limited gains and heavily in debt. They had, however, shown that Japan could defeat a major "Western" navy, destroying a Russian fleet in the Battle of the Straits of Tsushima.

In the Great War WWI, they acted as an arsenal for the Allies, ending the war with a full treasury and a much expanded munitions industry. They received the Gilbert and Marshall Islands, giving them strategic bases in the Pacific and expanding their "shield wall." However, they were totally ignored in the Peace Treaty negotiations, creating further resentment and animosity against "barbarians."

Preparing for the Great Pacific War

Preparation for their Great Pacific War began at the turn of the twentieth century, when the military dictated that all schools become military training grounds. Beginning in the earliest grades, male students would receive four hundred hours of military instruction, and all would be inculcated in the "ideals" selected by the military, a distorted version of the Bushido code.

The highly nationalistic curriculum stressed that the Japanese people were supreme, God-supported, and divine, led by the emperor, who was a god. The revised code subverted all loyalty directly to the emperor and, hence, the nation. It lacked any idea of protecting the weak, women, captives and non-Japanese. Rather, all non-Japanese peoples were to serve as docile servants and client nations—or exterminated if they proved uncooperative. Death in support of the emperor and nation was an admired and blessed thing, bringing great honor to one's family. It was considered the highest use of one's life—hence, the fanaticism of Japanese soldiers and suicidal charges.

In part because the Japanese never developed a western style "moral" sensitivity towards people other than themselves, the nation's conscience was vastly different from that of other countries. Even today, those executed for war crimes are honored because they, like samurai, gave their lives so that the emperor might be preserved, their war crimes ignored.

Hirohito, by his actions and acquiescence, encouraged violence both against non-Japanese and against Japanese political and military leaders who opposed his plans. History shows that Hirohito approved of the actions of his militarily led cabinets and armed forces, true to his grandfather Meiji. Ironically, he took the name of "Enlightened Peace."

Believing they were doing his will, so-called army renegade elements assassinated most of the outstanding civilian leaders opposed to war in 1921, 1932, 1936, and 1939. Corrupt political parties took turns, with the tacit approval of the military and war industries until, when Hirohito achieved control, they were joined into a rubber-stamp single party. Importantly, the military had a veto power in the government.

In 1931, the concept of "Hakao lehiu," meaning "bringing the eight corners (we would say four) of the world under one roof" (Japan's)—a quote purported to be from the first Japanese emperor—was adopted as a slogan of national policy. In 1939, Japan broadened the scope to the creation of a "Great Eastern Co-Prosperity Sphere."

With more years to prepare its people and without the hindrance of the Christian and Jewish religious populations faced by Hitler, Japan's leaders succeeded far better in making the state the center of culture and in creating an aggressive, ruthless military who were willing to die.

The Great Pacific War

The war began in 1931, when local army units, supposedly on their own initiative, moved into Manchuria. In 1932, they invaded Shanghai and the Jehol Province. Japanese textbooks began to show all of Asia and most of the Pacific as Japanese territory. As happened in Europe when Hitler grabbed adjacent countries, no one blinked, and only feeble protests were made. Even so, Japan walked out of the League of Nations in 1933 after the league voted to condemn her Manchurian aggression.

In 1937, the army promised a quick victory in China, and the world came to know of the Rape of Nanking and the killing of three hundred thousand civilians and raping of women down to the age of eleven.

Unfortunately for Japan, this story was published by Westerners living in Nanking (now Nanjing).

Japan's hopes for a quick Chinese victory evaporated in the depth of the vast country and the desperate measures taken by Chiang Kai-shek. It found itself in a quagmire, which consumed men and resources until the end of World War II, a front that could neither be won nor abandoned without loss of face.

In 1939, the Japanese Army clashed with the Soviet Army in an effort called "Strike North." It was soundly beaten in a modern tank battle at Nomonham in Outer Mongolia. This battle, where Soviet forces were led by General Zhukov, later a Russian leading general, presaged the better-known tank battles of World War II. Japan entered a treaty with Russia, and Stalin could use freed Soviet forces to divide Poland with Germany. Japan had been dealt two serious defeats, at Nomonham and in the bowels of central China. It had lost 185,000 soldiers, killed by the middle of 1941.

Japan turned to "Strike South," which would eventually involve the United States. What was not widely appreciated by the West was that endless fighting against a weak and divided Chinese army was not the only China solution. Capturing countries on its southern border would cut off aid and supplies, and Japan's military felt that China would fall into their grasp "like a ripe grape." Elsewhere the heightening tensions in 1940 and 1941 tended to be taken with a grain of salt against bigger European problems. So what if Japan took over Indochina (a Vichy France colony) on July 24, 1941?

The United States recognized the danger to the Philippines and started to reinforce their forces there with B-17s and additional troops to provide a base for war with Japan.

Why the Atrocities?

The theme that led Japan to World War II was the need to keep Japan "pure" by building an empire to buffer the superior people of Japan from the outside world—also a Hitler theme. From Emperor Komei to Hirohito, the theme that best explains the events of Japan's history is this effort to expand Japan's empire to keep the "white barbarians" at arm's length and outside Asia, to keep Japan safe with slave buffer states. This was the goal of administrations, military, and industry and, by virtue of Japan's social structure, her people.

Soldiers were toughened by participating in killing those who were "subhuman" in their extreme moral view on other peoples. The savagery exhibited by Japanese forces can then be traced to national goals; their training; their dedication to the emperor to the point of suicide; and, in many cases, the freedom to rampage by soldiers too long suppressed.

As David Bergamini in *Japan's Imperial Conspiracy* (1971) and Herbert Bix in *Hirohito and the Making of Modern Japan* (2000) show, the emperor was far from an uninformed figurehead, as post-WWII myth would claim. Invasions happened because he approved it. Atrocities could *not* have occurred without his knowledge.

But it is not possible to hate people so indoctrinated and led. They earnestly believed in the cause they had been taught because their belief had been bred into them, beginning as babies. As Jesus said, "Forgive them for they know not what they do."

And Japan's story is not the only story of atrocities and killings that stained the history of the twentieth century by people led by leaders with "a cause." It is not even the worst, just the one where such a large percentage of a nation's military were involved in horrors. Japan itself paid a steep price—the deaths of four million of her own people, a fifth of those who died in in the war in Asia.

APPENDIX 2
OUR FAMILY'S WAR YEARS CHRONOLOGY

1940
Summer/fall   After home leave to Akron, Ohio, we stopped in Tokyo, Yokohoma, Shanghai, and Hong Kong on the way back to the plantation.

1941
July   Assistant manager's wife and daughter return to the United States.

December 8   Pearl Harbor (Asian time). Father in Zamboanga buys canned food and medicine and draws money out of the bank. First US service man is killed on Mindanao.

1942
Spring   American refugees arrive from Zamboanga.
June 30   Japanese soldiers arrive at Pathfinder Plantation.

July 3	Taken to Zamboanga. After a short stay, we're sailed on a Japanese minesweeper to Davao (two days and nights) to "convent" assembly prison camp. We meet ten Bataan nurses.
August 23	Trucked to Happy Life Blues Internment Camp.

1943

June 16	My ninth birthday and the last shack I am allowed to help finish due to April 23 escape from Davao Penal Colony to bring word of atrocities and Bataan Death March to United States.
December 23	Told we're leaving for Manila and leave on December 24 in the hold of a freighter.

1944

January 2	Arrive at Santo Tomas Internment Camp (STIC).
January 10	Japan declares us "war prisoners" under Japanese War Prisoner Department—in other words, we're now POWs — not civilian internees.
February 1	Kenpeitai (Japan's military secret police) take over camp.
February 1	Families are allowed to live in shacks. We move in shortly afterward.
April 7	First transfer of personnel to Los Baños Camp.
April 30	Order is issued by commandant to clear twenty meters by the wall.

May 1	Sugar ration is cut in half to 10 grams (less than 0.4 oz.) per person per day.
May 15	Cereal ration is cut from 400 to 300 grams (11.5 oz.) per person per day.
June 10	Orders come to add one meter of barbed wire to that already on wall. Dad was on this "carpentry section" crew.
July 17	Prisoners are photographed in groups of five unrelated people and told all would be shot if any of the group escaped.
August 7	Japanese say there is no more toilet paper in all of the Philippines.
August 23	The Japanese commandant urges building air-raid shelters. Dad builds one under our shack.
September 15	Rice ration is cut from 300 to 250 grams (8.8 oz.) per day.
September 21	*First air raid* by US aircraft!
October 3	Ration is now 1,015 calories per day.
October 15	Air raid comes again, and the raids become more regular.
October 17	Guards take over part of second floor of the Education Building on the end across the street from our shack in addition to the lower floor below.
October 25	Camp goes to two meals a day due to lack of firewood and problems with the gas supply.

October 28	The Japanese start a garden in front of the Education Building.
November 1	Bowing practice at roll call is ordered.
November 15	A search is made of shack areas for the hidden radio.
December 5	Another 150 prisoners sent to Los Baños.
December 12	Cereal ration is cut to 210 grams (7.4 oz.) (to 200 grams on December 20—700 calories per day).
December 23	Lead internees are arrested. The first huge B-29s are seen.
December 25	Children get one small piece of hard candy and a banana. Leaflets drop with greetings from MacArthur—stiff penalties if found

1945

January 5	Four camp leaders are taken out of camp.
January 6	The Japanese burn records. I am given a rattle by one of the guards.
January 7	The Japanese move out supplies that had been brought into camp.
January 9	We watch a B-29 get shot down.
January 20	Shanty dwellers are allowed to bring chairs for roll call.
January 23	Lists were made of all men between the ages of eighteen and fifty.
January 28	Doctors are jailed for listing cause of death as starvation or malnutrition on death certificates.

February 2	Japanese burn records. I climb to the top of the Main Building to see fires
February 3	*Liberation*! It had been thirty-one months to the day and hour since we were put in prison. The 67 Japanese guards hole up in the Education Building across from us with 226 hostages. An American lieutenant is shot in the hand in a jeep in front of our shack, and we go to our air-raid shelter for a feast of 12-oz. can of Argentinian corned beef for our family of five. Battle of Manila starts!
February 5	Japanese guards march out with arms and flag between two lines of American 1st Cavalry soldiers.
February 6	Photo is taken of Barbara and me on the tank.
February 8	Fifteen are killed by Japanese shelling of the camp, one of whom I knew. A shell hits the Education Building. We are sleeping on cots behind the Education Building.
February 10	Two more are killed by Japanese shelling. Fifteen American soldiers and eight Filipinos are also killed.
February 12	Army nurses, including ten from Davao, leave to go home.
February 16	The photo on the tank appears in newspapers at home.
February 21	Bodies of camp leaders are found. All seamen from camp leave.

February 23	A memorial for camp leaders is held. Another 360 leave camp.
March 13	We leave camp, go to Clark Field, and return at the end of the day. We end up leaving on March 14, flying to Leyte (Tacloban convalescing camp).
April 24	We arrive in Akron via Biak Island, Hollandia and Finschaven, and New Guinea and San Francisco. President Roosevelt dies while we are on that sea.[ii]

BIBLIOGRAPHY

Abbitt, Raymond E., Rev. *A Light in the Darkness.* Privately printed, 2000.

———. Oral History North Texas University Oral History, Collection Number 282, February 25, 1975.

Bergamini, David. *Japan's Imperial Conspiracy: How Emperor Hirohito Led Japan into War against the West.* Morrow, 1971.

Boggs, Charles W. Jr., (Major USMC). *Marine Aviation in the Philippines.* Official Marine Publication, 1951.

Boyle, Helen Marie. *Gussie.* Angel Press, 1979.

Breuer, William B. *Retaking the Philippines.* St. Martin's Press, 1986.

Danner, Dorothy Still. *What a Way to Spend a War: Navy Nurse POs in the Philippines.* Naval Institute Press, 1995.

Davis, Wade. *One River.* Touchtone Books, 1996.

Dyess, William E. (Lt. Col.). *The Dyess Story.* G. P. Putnam's Sons, 1944.

Dyke, Thelma and Joyce Weidie. *Thelma's Diary, 1935.* AuthorHouse, 2013.

Frankel, Stanley A. *The 37th Infantry Division in World War II.* Infantry Journal Press, 1948.

Friedman, Kenneth I. *Afternoon of the Rising Sun.* Presidio Press, 2001.

Flanagan, E. M., Jr. SUA (Ret. Lt. Gen.). *The Los Baños Raid (and the 11th Airborne Jumps at Dawn).* Presidio Press, 1986.

Hartendorp, A.V.H. *The Santo Tomas Story,* McGraw Hill, 1964

Harris, Meirion and Susie. *Soldiers of the Sun: The Rise and Fall of the Imperial Japanese Army.* Random House, 1991.

Holland, Robert B. *The Rescue of Santo Tomas, Manila - WWII The Flying Column: 100 Miles to Freedom.* Turner Publishing, 2003.

———. *100 Miles to Freedom: The Epic Story of the Rescue of Santo Tomas and the Liberation of Manila, 1943–1945.* 2011.

Hoyt, Edwin P. *The Battle of Leyte Gulf.* Jove, 1972.

Holmes, Linda Goetz. *Unjust Enrichment.* Stackpole Books, 2001.

Hornfischer, James D. *The Last Stand of the Tin Can Sailors.* Bantam Books, 2004.

Huber, Joseph C., Jr. *Such a Life: The Autobiography of Thelma T. Huber Expanded by the Author.* AuthorHouse, 2014.

Lukacs, John D. *Escape from Davao.* Simon and Shuster, 2010.

Marshal, Cecily Mattocks. *Happy Life Blues.* Angus MacGregor Books, 2007.

Martin and Stephens. *Operation Plum.* Texas A&M Press, 2008.

McCall, James E. *Santo Tomas Internment Camp: STIC in Verse and Reverse: STIC-Toons and STIC-Tistics.* The Woodruff Printing Company, 1945.

McGee, John Hugh (Brigadier General, US Army, Ret.). *Rice and Salt: A History of the Defense and Occupation of Mindanao during World War II.* The Naylor Company, 1962.

Monahan, Evelyn M. and Rosemary Neidel-Greelee. *All This Hell: U.S. Nurses Imprisoned by the Japanese.* University Press of Kentucky, 2000. *All This Hell* gives the story of nurses on Luzon, including later events.

Morrison, Samuel Eliot. *The Liberation of the Philippines.* University of Illinois Press, 1959.

Norman, Elizabeth M. *We Band of Angels.* Random House, 1999.

Rees, Laurence. *Horror in the East: Japan and the Atrocities of World War II*. DA CAPO Press, 2001.

Reel, A Frank. *The Case of General Yamashita*. Kessinger Legacy Reprints of University of Chicago Press, 1949.

Salecker, Gene Eric. *Rolling Thunder Against the Rising Sun*. 2008.

Smith, Steven Trent. *The Rescue*. Wiley, 2001.

Stevens, Frederic H. *Santo Tomas*. Stratford House, 1946.

Wright, B. C. (Major). *The 1st Cavalry Division in World War II*. Toppan Printing Company Ltd. Tokyo, Japan, 1947.

NOTES

Chapter 1

[1] Linda Goetz Holmes, *Unjust Enrichment* (Stackpole Books, 2001), 103.

Chapter 3

[2] Joseph C. Huber, Jr. Such a Life: The Autobiography of Thelma T. Huber Expanded by the Author (AuthorHouse, 2014).

[3] Meirion and Susie Harris, *Soldiers of the Sun: The Rise and Fall of the Imperial Japanese Army* (Random House, 1991), 294. November 1941 as planned start of war from conference of November 1, 1940.

[4] Ibid, 295.

[5] Wade Davis, *One River* (Touchtone Books, 1996), 338; Hugh Allen *Rubber and the Goodyear Plantations* Goodyear, 1936), 212.

[6] Davis, *One River*, 341.

[7] Joyce Wiedie, *Thelma's Diary—1935* (AuthorHouse, 2013). The diary states that the room could easily use ten 9-by-12 rugs. My mother, Thelma Huber's, Cousin Thelma Dyke, whose diary was published, visited the plantation in late 1935.

Chapter 6

8   David Bergamini, Japan's Imperial Conspiracy: How Emperor Hirohito Led Japan into War against the West (Morrow, 1971), 132.

9   Brigadier General John Hugh McGee, US Army (Ret.), *Rice and Salt: A History of the Defense and Occupation of Mindanao during World War II* (The Naylor Company, 1962), 17.

Chapter 7

10   Elizabeth M. Norman, We Band of Angels (Random House, 1999), 157. Page 302 points out that they were told they were being repatriated and also gives the names of those who were with us at the Del Pilar Girls Seminary.

11   Evelyn M. Monahan and Rosemary Neidel-Greelee. *All This Hell: U.S. Nurses Imprisoned by the Japanese* (University Press of Kentucky, 2000). The book tells the story of nurses on Luzon, including later events

Chapter 8

12   Helen Marie Boyle, Gussie (Angel Press, 1979), 75. Happy Life Blues' main building was machined-gunned.

13   Ibid, 91.

14   Lt. Col William E. Dyess, *The Dyess Story*, G. P. Putnam's Sons, 1944); John D. Lukacs, *Escape from Davao* (Simon and Shuster, 2010).

Chapter 9

[15] Dyess, The Dyess Story.
[16] Lukacs, John D. *Escape from Davao.* Simon and Shuster, 2010. A map of the escape route shows its proximity to the plantation.
[17] www/wiki/Zamboanga. Also material from an anonymous unpublished history from military records of Mindanao, date unknown

Chapter 10

[18] Cecily Mattocks Marshal, Happy Life Blues (Angus MacGregor Books, 2007), 133. This account gives name of the ship to Manila. A web search reveals no record of a Shunsei Maru No. 1. Shinsei Maru No. 1 existed, but its sailing record does not match our trip.
[19] Father Raymond E. Abbitt, *A Light in the Darkness* (privately printed, n.d.), 45. Father Abbitt's account confirms my memory of singing Christmas carols in the hold of the Japanese maru taking us to Manila and includes lists of internees and examples of the rations he signed for to provide food for our camp, illustrating how meager they were.

Rev. Raymond E. Abbitt. Oral History, North Texas University, Oral History Collection, Number 282, February 25, 1975.

Chapter 11

[20] Fredric H. Stevens, Santo Tomas, (Stratford House, Inc. 1946), 389.
[21] Ibid, 445.
[22] Holmes, *Unjust Enrichment*, 101. Re: One package per month.

Chapter 12

[23] Stevens, Santo Tomas. The names of four leaders who were killed.
[24] Ibid. See the information regarding the death rate.
[25] Ibid, 480.

Chapter 13

[26] This discussion of the Battle of Leyte Gulf is based on a paper by the author presented to the Akron World War II and Korean War Round Table, based principally on the following:
- Edwin P. Hoyt, *The Battle of Leyte Gulf* (Jove, 1972).
- Kenneth I. Friedman, *Afternoon of the Rising Sun* (Presidio Press, 2001).
- Samuel Eliot Morrison, *The Liberation of the Philippines* (University of Illinois Press, 1959).
- James D. Hornfischer, *The Last Stand of the Tin Can Sailors* (Bantam Books, 2004).
- Discussion at WWII Round Table meeting with veteran who was an artilleryman on Leyte at the time.

Chapter 14

[27] Stevens, Santo Tomas, Calories per day
[28] James E. McCall, *Santo Tomas Internment Camp: STIC in Verse and Reverse: STIC-Toons and STIC-Tistics* (The Woodruff Printing Company, 1945).
[29] Stevens, *Santo Tomas*, menu.

Chapter 15

30 Lt. Col. Robert Ross Smith, Triumph in the Philippines, vol. 10 of The official War in the Pacific, a part of the US Army World War II, 1961, Library of Congress no. 62-60000, 240; Stanley A. Frankel, The 37th Division in World War II (Infantry Journal Press, 1948), 380. Yamashita and his chief of staff accepted no responsibility for the Battle of Manila and claimed that he had promised the Filipinos that battles would take place outside of Manila.

31 James M. Scott, *Rampage, MacArthur, Yamashita and the Battle of Manila* (W. W. Norton & Co. Inc., 2018).

Chapter 16

32 Holmes, Unjust Enrichment, 103.

33 Ibid (2000 Australians massacred); Laurence Rees, *Horror in the East: Japan and the Atrocities of World War II* (DA CAPO Press, 2001).

34 Gene Eric Salecker, *Rolling Thunder against the Rising Sun: The Combat History of the US Army Tank Battalions in the Pacific in WWII* (Stackpole Books, 2008), 273 and subsequent; Rees, *Horror in the East*.

35 Robert H. Holland, *100 Miles to Freedom: The Epic Story of the Rescue of Santo Tomas and the liberation of Manila 1943-1045 (Turner Publishing, 2011)*.

Chapter 17

36 Frankel, The 37th Division, 254. Frankel describes fires in the city requiring evacuation of these prisoners, who were initially also a risk from Japanese guns (447 civilians and 828 military prisoners at Bilibid).

37 Wright, *The 1ˢᵗ Cavalry Division in World War II* (Toppan Printing Company Ltd. 1947), 125. Wright records, "Tokyo, Japan—9 planes buzzed 'Role out the

Barrel, Santo Claus is coming Sunday or Monday and Battling Basic crashed gate.' (*The 1st Calvary Division* also lists major units and commanders.)

38 Major Charles W. Boggs, Jr. USMC, *Marine Aviation in the Philippines* (Official Marine Publication, 1951), appendix, table of aircraft (shows the use of SBD-6 as the aircraft listed variously); Holland, *100 Miles to Freedom*, 37.

39 Wright, *The 1st Calvary in World War II*, 132 "one mile from camp" and 130, which notes there were 67 Japanese soldiers and 267 prisoners in the Education Building (actually, there were 225 men and 1 woman visitor);

40 Frankel, *The 37th Division*. Frankel tells of the 37th taking over, and the tower of the Main Building taking nine hits and some thirty killed (since STIC records show fifteen, the balance must be soldiers).

41 William B. Breuer, *Retaking the Philippines* (St. Martin's Press, 1896), 152–53 and photos after page 180 of Japanese and Americans marching together and of the destruction of Manila, on which no bombs were dropped.

42 Holland, *100 Miles*.

Chapter 19

43 Stevens, Santo Tomas, 482. Some one hundred were also wounded, a casualty rate of 3 percent, and over 5 percent when starvation deaths after liberation are included.

44 Ibid

45 Wright, *The 1st Calvary*. On the fifth, the 37th took over.

46 Frankel, *The 37th Division*, 239, and a separate booklet put out by the 37th. The 37th "nearly got to Manila first" (in other words, ahead of the 1st Cavalry). Page 242 lists Japanese atrocities in Manila. Page 249 states that the Japanese defenses were oriented south not north. Page 250 notes that Manila was the *only major city* taken from the Japanese. Page 255 states that the 1st Cavalry and we at Santo Tomas were cut off and that MacArthur had to postpone his visit to Santo Tomas until a path was cleared by the 37th, who broke through

to "rescue" the 1st Cavalry and Santo Tomas. Page 296 notes that the 37th, the 11th Airborne, and the 1st Cavalry fought the Battle of Manila and the 37th killed 13,006 Japs of 16,665 killed.

Chapter 20

[47] Dorothy Still Danner, What a Way to Spend a War: Navy Nurse POs in the Philippines (Naval Institute Press, 1995).

[48] The description of this chapter is based on stories I heard in camp at the time. And for its details, I relied on the excellent book by Lt. Gen. E. M. Flanagan, Jr. SUA (Ret.), *The Los Baños Raid: And the 11th Airborne Jumps at Dawn* (Presidio Press, 1986).

Chapter 23

[49] Capt. J. U. Ladaman, Jr. USN (Ret.) December, 1973 Naval Institue Proceedings Re: US Goldstar.

Epilogue

[50] *Life*, May 21, 1945.

Appendix 1

[51] This appendix was written based on a study of the following: W. G. Beasley, *The Rise of Modern Japan* (St. Martin's Press, 1990); David Bergamini, *Japan's Imperial Conspiracy: How Emperor Hirohito led Japan into War against the West* (Morrow, 1971), 1,399 (according to archeologists, Jimmu did not reign in 660 BC but in first century AD); Herbert P. Bix, *Hirohito and the Making of Modern Japan* (Harper Collins, 2000); Iris Chang, *The Rape of Nanking: The Forgotten*

Holocaust of World War II (Basic Books, 1997); Bernard M. Cohen, PhD, and Maurice C. Cooper, MD, *A Follow-up Study of World War II Prisoners of War* (government publication, September 21, 1954), 27 (891 of every 1,000 former prisoners of the Japanese required hospitalization after release as compared to 248 out of every 1,000 of those who were prisoners in Europe); Stuart D. Goldman, *Nomonhan, 1939* (Naval Institute Press, 2012); Haruko Taya Cook and Theodore F. Cook, *Japan at War: An Oral History* (The New Press, 1992); William Craig, *The Fall of Japan* (Dell, 1967); Peter Duns, *Modern Japan*, 2nd ed. (Houghton Mifflin Company, 1998); Robert B. Edgerton, *Warriors of the Rising Sun* (W. W. Norton and Company, 1997); Bernard Edwards, *Blood and Bushido: Japanese Atrocities at Sea 1941–1945* (Brick Towers Press, 1991); Frank Gibney, ed., *Letters to the Editor of Asahi Shimbun Senso: The Japanese Remember the Pacific War.* Translated by Beth Cary (M. E. Sharpe, 1995); Grant K. Goodman, ed., *Japanese Cultural Policies in Southeast Asia during World War 2* (Saint Martin Press, 1991); Michael J. Goodwin, *Shobun: A Forgotten War Crime in the Pacific* (Stackpole Books, 1995); Meirion and Susie Harris, *Soldiers of the Sun: The Rise and Fall of the Imperial Japanese Army* (Random House, 1991); Saburo Ienaga, *The Pacific War 1931–1945* (Pantheon Books, 1979); Jintaro Ishida, *The Remains of War: Apology and Forgiveness: Testimonies of the Japanese Imperial Army and Its Filipino Victims* (The Lyons Press, 2001); Samuel Eliot Morrison, *Breaking the Bismarck's Barrier* (Little Brown, 1950) (shows the strategic value of the Gilberts and Marshall Islands to Japan); Nihon no Ichiban Nagai Hi, *Japan's Longest Day* (compiled by the Pacific War Research Society Kodansha International, Ltd. Tokyo, Japan, 1965) (details the attempted coup against the Emperor just prior to Japan's surrender); Laurence Rees, *Horror in the East: Japan and the Atrocities of World War II* (DA CAPO Press, 2001); A. Frank Reel, *The Case of General Yamashita* (Kessinger Legacy Reprints of University of Chicago Press, 1949) (an attempt to defend Yamashita); Robert Ross, *Triumph in the Philippines: The War in the Pacific* (Office of the Chief of Military History Dept. of the Army, Washington DC 1963 Library of Congress 62-60000.), 92 (addresses Yamashita's unwillingness to fight in Manila); Dan Van der Vat, *The Pacific Campaign* (Simon & Shuster, 1991).

An alternate view is given in Eria Hotta, *Japan 1941: Countdown to Infamy* (Alfred A Knopf, 2013). The author tries to shift the blame from Emperor Hirohito and Tojo by focusing on "runaway junior officers," Japanese culture, myths about the powerlessness of the emperor and the feeble attempts by some to head off war. Hotta does not address the emperor's actions between 1931 and Pearl Harbor; nor does she talk about the morality of Japan's actions from 1931.

CPSIA information can be obtained
at www.ICGtesting.com
Printed in the USA
LVHW110745280221
679631LV00062B/1035/J